MEDIEVAL WELSH LYRICS

Joseph P. Clancy

MEDIEVAL WELSH LYRICS

MACMILLAN
London · Melbourne · Toronto

ST MARTIN'S PRESS
New York
1965

MACMILLAN AND COMPANY LIMITED
Little Essex Street London WC2
also Bombay Calcutta Madras Melbourne

THE MACMILLAN COMPANY OF CANADA LIMITED
70 Bond Street Toronto 2

ST MARTIN'S PRESS INC
175 Fifth Avenue New York 10010 NY

Library of Congress Catalogue Card No : 65-22792

891.66C
C 527

PRINTED IN GREAT BRITAIN

CONTENTS

v

CONTENTS

CONTENTS

INTRODUCTION

POETRY, said Robert Frost, is what gets lost in translation. He was right, of course ; but there is another side to it. Some poetry gets lost, for most of us, without translation. The Welsh poetry of the Middle Ages, one of the richest bodies of Western lyric, is little known outside Wales itself, for lack of much or adequate translation.

This book provides translations in verse of more than one hundred of these poems. It does not attempt to cover the entire medieval period, nor to represent all forms of lyric. It is restricted in time to the later Middle Ages, and, with one exception, to one verse form, the *cywydd deuair hirion*. These restrictions are less severe than they sound, and work, I believe, to the advantage of readers who have not previously encountered Medieval Welsh poetry. The great age of the Welsh lyric is from 1340 to 1620,[1] and during it, 'although there were many metrical patterns of every kind at the call of the bards, the finest craftsmen preferred the *cywydd* to any other'.[2] And subjects and themes have a wider range, with greater immediate appeal to the modern reader, in these centuries than in the preceding ones.

It is, at first glance, remarkable that Wales produced its greatest poetry after 1282, when Llywelyn ap Gruffudd, still called 'our last Prince' by the Welsh, fell in battle against Edward I. Wales was truly 'no wretched scrap of territory, spent and exhausted, ... but a country whose self-consciousness was sufficiently alive and whose traditions were sufficiently

---

[1] This may seem to extend far beyond the medieval period, but the Middle Ages were slow to die in Wales, and the Welsh literary historian usually treats the poetry in this book under a single heading, though allowing for signs of change at the end of the period.

[2] Thomas Parry, *A History of Welsh Literature*, translated by H. Idris Bell (Oxford, 1955), p. 140.

1

well-established to hold for centuries afterwards, indeed until
the present moment'.¹ But some credit should be given to
Edward, too ; while he built the great castles at Conway,
Caernarvon, Harlech, Criccieth, and Beaumaris to keep the
rebellious North firmly under English control, divided the
country into shires and imposed on it the English administrative structure, and established trading-towns peopled with
English colonists, he otherwise, as Sir Arthur Bryant states,
'left Wales much as he found it. ... He left [the Welsh] —
the most precious thing of all — their language and, with a few
exceptions, their Welsh officers and chieftains to fill the English
legal and administrative posts. . . . He left them, in other
words, not a Welsh State, which under provocation he had
taken from them, but the wherewithal of Welsh nationhood.'²

In the centuries after the Conquest Welsh soldiers served
in the English armies against Scotland and France (the longbow
that won at Crécy was in origin a Welsh weapon), Welsh
chieftains built their manor houses after the latest English
styles, and many Welshmen were drawn into the commercial
life of the towns. But hostility towards the English flickered
through these years, to blaze up in the brief glory of Owain
Glyn Dŵr's rebellion (1400–1410). And it was this hostility
that brought so many Welshmen to support Henry, grandson
of Owen Tudor of Anglesey, against Richard III. Ironically,
it was Henry VIII, son of 'the Welsh king', who struck the
severest blow to Welsh cultural independence : after the Act
of Union in 1536, English was made the sole official language
of Wales.

The poetry that remains from these centuries is a mirror
of the world that gave it birth, but a distorting mirror. It
reflects the hills and wooded valleys, the birds and beasts, the
life of the courts that welcomed the bards, but we glimpse
only seldom the life of the farms and of the towns.

What remains today is the entertainment of the upper stratum of
society — the nobility, men to whom the nation owes a great debt

---

¹ Parry, *Welsh Literature*, p. 44.
² *The Age of Chivalry* (New York, 1964), p. 92.

as the upholders of civilization, though some of them were fiercely quarrelsome, lax in their morals, and oppressive to the poor. They varied in respect of their wealth, but they all owned some land, dwelt in comfortable houses, at their best protected and helped the poor, took pride in their lineage from son to father and grandfather and great-grandfather, lived luxuriously, many of them, on the choicest food of the country and the liquors of the Continent, and above all formed a class of lettered men who derived pleasure from the reading of poetry or from hearing it recited.[1]

It is a world long gone. But as we read its poems,

> Stones to the walls fly back,
> The gay manors are full
> Of music ; the poets return
> To feast at the royal tables.[2]

The modern reader often brings to the poetry of other ages an attitude that is a barrier to his understanding and enjoyment. He is eager to find the 'individual' and impatient with the 'conventional'. But for the medieval Welsh bard, his essential task was not exploration but celebration, not the sensitive revelation of self at a single historical moment, but the enactment of permanently valid ritual. Within this, we can distinguish some quite individual voices, but it is wisest to approach this poetry by attempting to understand its conventions and to cultivate a taste for ritual well performed.

The *cywydd* as a verse form was an innovation in fourteenth-century Wales, and its introduction accompanied an expansion of the subjects and themes thought fit for bardic treatment. But it is continuously and chiefly employed through the later Middle Ages for the oldest of bardic functions, the eulogy of noble patrons. Siôn Tudur's poem on the bards shows clearly how this was still thought of, at the end of the sixteenth century, as their chief function :

> Praising the blood of thousands,
> Princes and swift-riding knights ;

---

[1] Parry, *Welsh Literature*, pp. 128–9.
[2] R. S. Thomas, 'On Hearing a Welshman Speak', *Poetry for Supper* (London, 1958), p. 16.

> Lords of the scent of learning,
> Mighty bishops in our midst ;
> Fruitful, generous chieftains,
> Bearers of the ancient blood. . . .

Social change has made it difficult for us to approach the eulogies impartially, or with much hope of pleasure. What self-respecting modern poet, as his chief task, eulogizes the dean of a college, the bishop of a diocese, the local captains of industry, the mayors of various cities, and the president or prime minister of his country ? There are, too, the barriers of unfamiliar names of persons and places and the tracing of ancestry, things that must have made the poems of immediate appeal as they were sung in the great halls, but that leave us, if not bewildered, cold.

For the latter problems, I know no solution but a saturation in Welsh history and geography, a bit much to expect of the general reader. The former, the initial prejudice, is a different matter. It is well to keep in mind that much of this poetry is *by* noblemen as well as *for* them, and that any image we have of sycophantic bard flattering simple-minded lord is, to say the least, distorted. Dr. Parry notes that 'it is clear that the craft of poetry was familiar enough to the nobility throughout the centuries, and that they partook very liberally, quite as a matter of everyday routine, in the literary activity of their age. . . . Poetry was not the interest of a small select circle of connoisseurs, but a thing pervading a large section of the lettered class ; and it is to be remembered that these lesser nobles were very numerous.'[1] All of this, of course, is no guarantee of the 'sincerity' of a poem, but sincerity is a very hard test to apply. We might agree, at least, that our judgment should be made on how the poem itself behaves, rather than on what we know or suspect of its subject from other sources of information. And we should realize that Iolo Goch's appreciation of the court of Owain Glyn Dŵr is not necessarily less heartfelt than Dafydd ap Gwilym's appreciation of Dyddgu's beauty, nor Guto'r Glyn's lament for Siôn ap Madog

[1] *Welsh Literature*, p. 136.

Pilstwn less rooted in a real sense of loss than Llywelyn Goch's for his sweetheart or Lewis Glyn Cothi's for his five-year-old son.

Having said this, I must confess that my arguments are against a prejudice I share, and that there are fewer eulogies and elegies for patrons in this book than there should be for a picture of this body of poetry in its proper proportions. Enough have been included, however, to give the reader some notion of what these poems are like, and to suggest, in Iolo Goch's eulogy of Sir Hywel, for example, or Gruffudd Gryg's elegy for Rhys ap Tudur, how very fine they can be. History and social change add interest to some of these poems : echoes of the Wars of the Roses in Guto'r Glyn's praise of Wiliam Herbart and, on the Lancastrian side, Tudur Penllyn's of Dafydd ap Siancyn, and of the break-up of the feudal order and the encroachments of English law in Tudur Aled's 'A Plea for Peace'.

I have included two poems of protest against bardic abuses, and the difference between them is worth noting. Siôn Cent, at the beginning of the fifteenth century, attacks eulogistic lies on grounds quite different from those of Siôn Tudur at the end of the sixteenth. For the former, the abuse is in hyperbole and an excessive love of the world and its goods, while for the latter the abuse is in applying the rituals of praise to newly rich social upstarts, who crave the honours but lack the merits of the old aristocracy.

In that poem, Siôn Tudur notes as the first function of the bard 'praising God before all others', and it is hardly surprising to find many devotional lyrics in this period. As in English devotional poetry of the same age, the poet speaks less as an individual than as the voice of the Christian community, praising Christ, the Blessed Virgin, and the saints, confessing man's sinfulness and praying for forgiveness, as in Gruffudd Gryg's 'Christ the King' and Huw Cae Llwyd's 'The Cross'. A more individual note may be heard in the work of Siôn Cent. In his whole-hearted dedication to lyrics of moral meditation and religious praise he is unique among

the *cywyddwyr*, but even in his work, the meditations on
mortality and sin are in a very traditional medieval vein, and
are strikingly similar to English poetry of the same period.
Guto'r Glyn, on the other hand, writes from a genuinely
personal setting in the devotional poems of his old age, though
the conventions of eulogy to a patron and pious celebration
are still present.

What we are apt to think of as unquestionably personal,
the love lyric, was also poetry for public performance, as
it had been from the time of the troubadours. But it is going
rather far to say that this kind of poetry 'is only a pretence,
an opportunity for the poets to show their skill in intricacy
of metre and conciseness of statement'.[1] What is true of the
lyrics to patrons is true here : a public poetry may have
personal roots, or it may express a general pattern of human
experience or an ideal without being 'insincere'. Too much
stress seems to me to be laid by many commentators on the
'artificiality' of courtly love and its hyperbolic praises and
complaints. I would suggest that for many an adolescent
first experiencing love and many an older lover enduring an
absence from his beloved these poems provide a truer statement of at least some of their feelings than it is fashionable to
admit.

Courtly love had entered Welsh lyric, as an influence from
France, well before the fourteenth century. The reader will
recognize many of its conventions in these poems : love at
first sight, the imagery of fever and sickness, the married state
of the lady. One finds in Dafydd ap Gwilym's lyrics all the
stages of advancement in love, from the first awestruck
awakening of love in the lover's heart to his praise of the lady's
beauty and complaints of her unkindness, to acceptance as a
suitor and, finally, to sexual consummation. But there is far
more than this in Dafydd : he is as uniquely, single-mindedly
dedicated to the pursuit of love as Siôn Cent is to religion.
He does write some poems to patrons and some on devotional
themes, but the bulk of his poetry delights in his many-sided

[1] Parry, *Welsh Literature*, p. 155.

experience of love for Morfudd — and for others. Particularly
notable in Dafydd is the humour he often brings to this
experience : if he can sing sweetly and tenderly, he can also
denounce in comic frenzy the obstacles to love's fulfilment,
and can find in himself the chief figure of fun. And if he has
his limits, if he cannot touch the experience of anguish in
Llywelyn Goch's lament, for example, or give us, any more
than his contemporaries or successors do, the inner tensions
of Shakespeare or Donne, he has a wider range and at times
a greater depth of feeling than some of his critics have con-
ceded him. The tradition of courtly love does not move, in
Dafydd or the other bards, to a Christian platonization ;
rather it alternates or blends with the earthier attitudes of the
Goliards and of Ovid, whom Dafydd rightly names as his
master and of whom he often reminds us.

Lyrics of nature do not form a really separate category.
There are a few exceptions, such as Gruffudd ab Adda's *cywydd*
to the birch, but in general nature appears as a background
in the love poems. 'Background' is not quite the proper
word : in many of the lyrics, the lady may not be exactly
an afterthought, but love for her allows the poet to dwell on
the beauties of the grove to which he invites her or the creature
he sends her as a *llatai*, a messenger of love. It is in Dafydd ap
Gwilym, once again, that we find the fullest response to nature
among these poets, a response it is tempting to call peculiarly
Celtic, if one knows earlier Welsh and Irish poetry. The
nature of this response can be defined partly by negatives :
it is not a sense of divine immanence or transcendence or of
nature as an allegorical or analogical mirror. Nature is
responded to, rather, in itself, sometimes for itself and sometimes as a participant in human actions ; it is responded to
as a fellow-creature, sometimes delightful and sometimes
exasperating. It is, in fact, a thoroughly if unconsciously
Christian response, though one not often found in Christian
poetry.

Poems to fellow bards form a rather special group among
these lyrics. It was customary for the bards to engage in

B

contentions, humorously, as in the exchange of poems included
here between Llywelyn ap Gutun and Guto'r Glyn, or with
what seems a half-seriousness, as in Gruffudd Gryg's objections
to the excesses of Dafydd ap Gwilym's love songs, or with
the bitter seriousness of Siôn Cent's strictures to Rhys Goch
Eryri on bardic follies. It was a matter of compliment, too,
for one bard to write an elegy for another *before* the latter's
death, though I believe none of the elegies I have included
were so written. Dr. Parry calls the elegies on fellow bards
'among the most sincere poems of the period',[1] but I wonder
if this sense of sincerity does not come, very often, from our
knowing the dead poet from his works as we cannot know
the dead patron, and so feeling that the praise and mourning
are justified.

The various kinds of *cywyddau*, of praise, of mourning,
of petition, of description, of love, and of contention, are
represented in my selection. I have tried to make that selection
reflect the full range of experience and response in this body
of lyric, from sombre brooding on the decay of flesh to the
vision of everlasting glory, from the genial pleasures of court
to the grimness of battle to sheep-dealing and seafaring, from
exuberant delight in bird and beast to vexation with the
weather, from praise of a mistress' eyebrow to joyful love-
making to bawdy knockabout farce. And I have deliberately
selected certain lyrics to show the variations skilful *cywyddwyr*
could play on a familiar theme through these centuries.

In the case of four poets, my selection has been similarly
motivated. Dafydd ap Gwilym has, of course, pride of place :
that more than one-third of the poems I have included are
his is no more than a reflection of his unquestioned position
as the greatest of Welsh poets, and I wished to show his
thematic range and variations on single themes as fully as
possible. But though Dafydd is the greatest, he is by no means
the most representative of bards, and I have tried in his contemporaries, Iolo Goch and Gruffudd Gryg, to give a cross-
section of the typical bard's body of work. With Guto'r

[1] *Welsh Literature*, p. 153.

Glyn, a century later, I have again tried to suggest the variety and individual voice of this bard, and to show how his lyrics reflect both continuity and change in the development of the medieval lyric.

I have included a reasonable number of other bards, and suggested, where more than one poem from a bard is included, something of his range. The selection reflects in its proportions the rich output of the later fourteenth and the fifteenth centuries, and the decrease in verse of high quality by the end of the sixteenth. But I cannot claim that the number of lyrics chosen from a poet's work is a fair guide to his achievement, or that every good poet of the period is represented. For all my attempts to be conscientious, certain poems were translated because I found myself attracted to them or because they were more readily available than others ; some are not here because of personal distaste or my inability to translate them, their inaccessibility in satisfactory texts, or, quite simply, my ignorance of their existence. For my selection, as well as my translation, can hardly help but reflect some of the arbitrariness, rashness, and ignorance of the amateur, though I hope it reflects the enthusiasm as well.

In structure — by which I mean the pattern of thoughts and feelings, what corresponds in lyric to plot in narrative — the *cywyddau* often differ strikingly from traditional Western lyric. We may loosely divide the familiar modes of lyric structure into 'logical', in which the basic activity imitated in the poem is the working of the conscious mind thinking out a matter or presenting an argument, as in Marvell's 'To His Coy Mistress', and 'associative', in which the activity imitated is the rapid movement from one set of thoughts and feelings to another in a moment of intense excitement, as in Donne's 'The Canonization', or the drifting movement of reverie, as in Yeats's 'Among School Children'. We can find both modes of structure in some of the *cywyddau* ; we can even find in a few a narrative rather than a lyric base. But in others, either in whole poems or long sections, these modes are not used, and if we come to them expecting a 'plotted' movement to a climax, we may conclude, as H. Idris Bell does, that this poetry 'suffers from a lack of the architectonic quality', that the bards have concentrated on details and 'have frequently neglected the task of so organizing and correlating the various parts of a composition as to give it an internal unity of design'.[1]

The best illustration of this is in the poems made up almost entirely of descriptive and metaphoric images, for a gift requested from a patron, as in Tudur Aled's 'The Stallion' and Lewis Glyn Cothi's 'The Coverlet', for a love-messenger, as in Dafydd ap Gwilym's 'The Wind', or simply for an object of affection, as in Llywelyn ap y Moel's praise of his woodland hideout, or of detestation, as in Iolo Goch's 'The Ship'. Occasional passages of description and metaphor may fit very well into the other modes of lyric structure, but the whole point of these poems is the series of images, and there is, for the most part, no feeling that one couplet must be where it is in the poem, no sense of moving through a sequence of thoughts and feelings each of which flows naturally from the other. And this apparent lack of an overall design, though not of a central focus, is present in other *cywyddau* than those devoted to description : what we get is at times a 'spiralling', at times a 'radial' structure, rather than a 'progressive' one. As I try to think of parallels in English lyric, all that comes to mind are Smart's 'A Song to David' and most of Crashaw's works.[2]

The mention of Crashaw leads me to suggest one explanation of this mode of structure. Crashaw is sometimes read as if he were a kind of failed Donne or Herbert, whereas his essential difference from his two predecessors lies in his being,

---

[1] *The Development of Welsh Poetry* (Oxford, 1936), p. 5.

[2] George Herbert's sonnet 'Prayer' and many of Henry Vaughan's lyrics show the direct influence of this Welsh mode of lyric structure, as do passages in Hopkins and Dylan Thomas. I suspect the 'Welshness' of Thomas's techniques is largely derived from Hopkins, who had studied both the language and the poetry. (See W. H. Gardner, 'G. Manley Hopkins as a *Cywyddwr*', *Transactions of the Honourable Society of Cymmrodorion* (1940), pp. 184–188.)

what is rare among English poets, a poet of celebration rather than exploration. The stance of celebration (or its opposite, denunciation) gives the poet a special kind of perspective, one in which a process in time, on which both logical and associative lyrical structures are based, is unimportant, in which all aspects of the central, celebrated thing matter equally and are to be perceived simultaneously. I offer this simply as a theory, one way of accounting for the structural peculiarities of so many of the *cywyddau* (present in the earlier Welsh lyric as well), and of helping the reader to allow them to assume their own form rather than the form he may expect.[1]

One smaller feature of *cywydd* structure must also be noted, one that provides a peculiar problem for the translator, and, in the solution I have attempted, a problem for the reader as well. This is the use of *sangiad*, a break or syntactic sidestep in the flow of the sentence. A simple illustration is in the finale of Dafydd ap Gwilym's poem on his failure with the girls of Llanbadarn :

> O dra disgwyl, dysgiad certh,
> Drach 'y nghefn, drych anghyfnerth,
> Neur dderyw ym, gerddrym gâr,
> Bengamu heb un gymar.

In the first three lines the forward movement of the sentence is concentrated into the first half of each line, the second half providing a kind of parenthetical commentary :

> From too much looking, strange lesson,
> Backwards, sight of weakness,
> It happened to me, strong song's friend,
> To bow my head without one companion.

This is a fairly simple example of a constantly used device.

---

[1] Gwyn Williams in his foreword to *The Burning Tree* (London, 1956) has a brief treatment of this question. 'The absence of a centred design, of an architectural quality,' he insists, 'is not a weakness in old Welsh poetry but results quite reasonably from a specific view of composition' (p. 15). He goes on to note that our structural assumptions are largely the result of conditioning by the Greco–Roman tradition, and to cite parallels in Celtic art and architecture to this mode of lyric structure.

The opening lines of Iolo Goch's poem to the ploughman provide a more complex one :

> Pan ddangoso, rhyw dro rhydd,
> Pobl y byd, peibl lu bedydd,
> Garbron Duw, cun eiddun oedd,
> Gwiw iaith ddrud, eu gweithredoedd,
> Ar ben Mynydd, lle bydd barn,
> I gyd, Olifer gadarn,
> Llawen fydd, chwedl diledlaes,
> Llafurwr, tramwywr maes.

Literally, the sequence of lines and phrases is this :

> When show, a time of freedom,
> The world's people, lively throng of the baptized,
> In God's presence, lord of desire he was,
> Bold proper language, their deeds,
> On top of Mount, where there will be judgment,
> All, strong Olivet,
> Cheerful will be, joyful story,
> The ploughman, traverser of a field.

In no line does the sentence flow uninterruptedly, and there are particularly drastic breaks between closely related words, 'deeds' and 'all', 'Mount' and 'Olivet', a device known as *trychiad*. How much of this should the translator keep ? More importantly, how much *can* he keep without producing a hopeless syntactic tangle ? It may be noted here that even for those born to Welsh the rhetorical devices make some of the *cywyddau* very difficult to read.

This raises the question of the bards' purposes in using *sangiad* and *trychiad*. The explanation given by Dr. Parry is that these originated as 'metrical phrases, elements put into the poem not for the sake of the meaning but for that of the metre, and ... it must be remembered about Welsh poetry that it attaches as much honour to metre as to thought'.[1] The translator may therefore see no reason for preserving this feature of structure, and most previous translators have not seriously attempted to do so. But the effects of *sangiad*, at

[1] *Welsh Literature*, p. 146.

least in the best lyrics, are more than merely metrical, even though this was the original reason for its use. One does find, frequently enough, that the *sangiadau* are riddling or almost meaningless, but they often produce a peculiar effect of multiplicity, of continuous parenthetical comment simultaneous with the development of the main theme of the *cywydd*. This is certainly true in Dafydd ap Gwilym's lines quoted above, and in the last part of Dafydd's 'The Rival' what at first seems an exasperating abuse of the device in the *sangiadau* comparing Morfudd's complexion to foam is justified in suggesting the obsession of the overwrought lover. One can note, too, the effectiveness of *sangiad* in heightening the farcical confusion in Dafydd's 'In a Tavern'. And in general, *sangiad* slows down the movement of what, given a sevensyllable line, might otherwise be an unsuitably rapid flow ; it adds a needed weight and dignity, as in the passage quoted from Iolo Goch.

I find that, for myself at least, omitting the *sangiad* effect in a translation produces excessive speed and lightness and a curious flatness, that something vital to the original has been lost. I have therefore taken the risk of trying to reproduce it wherever possible. Sometimes, of course, the use of *sangiad* and particularly of *trychiad* could not be rendered without producing a wild confusion in English. One does grow accustomed to the device, I find, especially if one tries to hear the poems (which were, after all, oral compositions), with pauses in the voice for the *sangiadau*. It may be some consolation to the reader who finds himself bewildered at his first encounter with a passage, that his experience mirrors that of a reader of the original. And let me reassure a possibly discouraged reader that the frequency of *sangiadau* varies from poet to poet and poem to poem, that many of the lyrics offer no serious difficulties, and that, in any case, obscurities caused by the device are of the surface not of the depths, complexities of expression more than of feeling, and the reader's failure to see relevance or even meaning in a particular phrase will often be shared by the Welsh reader and the translator and seldom

mars the enjoyment of the poem as a whole. I trust I have
not at any point inadvertently created difficulties not in the
original poem.

I have tried to capture in these translations the exuberance,
fancifulness, and epigrammatic point of the originals, their
descriptive exactness and freshness as well as their frequent
use — a convention of oral poetry — of stock adjectives and
phrases. But one feature of style that I have been unable to
reproduce adequately is the use of compound words, constant
in the fourteenth-century bards as a stylistic heritage from
their predecessors, less frequent a technique in the later bards.
The opening line of Dafydd ap Gwilym's 'The Wave', 'Y don
bengrychlon grochlais,' can be rendered with English compounds as 'Curlytopped loudcrying wave,' but his address to
the seagull as 'esgudfalch edn bysgodfwyd' ('swift-proud bird
fish-fed'), creates more of a problem : 'fishfeeding' will do,
but can one compound in English, as these poets constantly
do in Welsh, such adjectives as 'swift-proud' ? In general I
have compounded where I could do so comfortably, and
occasionally compounded where the Welsh does not in an
attempt to make up in slight measure for the many times I
have destroyed a compound in translation. One source of
pleasure in the Welsh is certainly lost, and one major stylistic
change during these centuries is obscured for the reader, but
I see no help for it.

One further note on style, before I turn to the subject of
rhythm and music. A student at Aberystwyth, when told I
was translating these poems into English, asked pointedly,
'Which English ?' The only answer, I suppose, is 'my own'.
I have not tried to cultivate an 'Anglo-Welsh' style, and I have
not thought it wise to attempt to imitate the archaic, poetic
diction frequent in the originals. (The temptation, in using
a very short line, to the use of "neath', 'ere', etc. was very
great, but I cannot employ such words comfortably. Nor
can I, in a poem of real anguish, translate 'Gwae fi' as 'Woe's
me' — my ways of avoiding this may well amuse those who

know the poems at first hand. Such a word as 'churl', on the
other hand, offers little choice : it is used by these poets with
the strong sense of its social meaning, and there is simply no
modern equivalent.) I have used my own American English
as the basic 'voice' through which the poems come, heightened
where I found it necessary or possible : the modern translator
tends often to be excessively colloquial, to fight shy of heightened style, and while I share these faults, I have tried to
minimize them. I have walked as carefully as my limitations
allow the line between unpoetic literalness and poetic liberal-
ity : I translate as a means of writing poetry, but I am attempting 'translation', in so far as this is really possible, not
'imitation'.

'Nothing which is set in harmony by the bond of music,'
wrote Dante, 'can be transferred from its own language to
another without destroying all its sweetness and harmony.'
And in the Welsh poetic tradition 'sound is as important as
sense'.[1] A vital decision for the translator of lyric is his choice
of metrical and musical patterns, the attempt to reproduce
some of these features in the original or the resort to patterns
of his own. I do not know how different readers react to
this — certainly some are content as long as the translation
gives pleasure, however distant its harmonies from those of
what is translated. Myself, I require at least a certain neutrality
of effect : some of Rolfe Humphries's excellent renderings
of Ovid disturb me because they are sonnets, and I cannot
associate that form with Latin verse.

The Welsh *cywydd deuair hirion* uses a line seven syllables
long, and a couplet in which one end-rhyme is stressed, the
other unstressed, e.g. lovers-hers, men-happen. Translators
have most often chosen to use the English tetrameter couplet
as the closest equivalent to this. But I see no reason, given the
frequent use of syllabic metre in modern English verse, for
not adopting the seven-syllable line, and I have done so. The
nature of the Welsh language, which expresses the indefinite

[1] Parry, *Welsh Literature*, p. 48.

article by omitting the definite and which can express a genitive relationship by word order alone, and the use of compounds previously mentioned, allow more to be contained in the short line than is always possible in the English equivalent, and I have been forced to omit adjectives sometimes and whole phrases on a few occasions. But I think that by keeping within a metrical framework that demands conciseness and point I have produced better poems and ones closer to the Welsh in their effects that I could have with a longer, looser line. I have not used rhyme : normal English rhyme destroys the rhythms of the *cywydd* couplet, the *cywydd* rhyme is very alien to an English ear, and in either case too much distortion of the sense would have been necessary. Instead I have used a couplet with one stressed and one unstressed final syllable : the overall effect is of couplet pattern, and can capture to a considerable extent the movement of the Welsh couplet. I have made no attempt to make these line-endings correspond in stress or the lack of stress with the particular couplets of each poem, but have rather sought a general effect close to that of *cywydd* pattern. It should be possible to detect in the translations the tendency of the bards to move from the freer use of run-on lines and couplets in the fourteenth century to the tightly epigrammatic and self-contained couplets of the fifteenth, a development similar to that in the English pentameter couplet from Jonson and Donne to Dryden and Pope. I have tried, as frequently as linguistic differences would allow, to mirror the movement of sentence and phrase in the Welsh, the general flow of the original lyric, though distortion of this was often a practical necessity.

The least solvable problem the *cywydd* poses the translator is its use of *cynghanedd*, strict patterns of alliteration and internal rhyme.[1] There are three basic forms of *cynghanedd* : *cynghanedd gytsain*, which uses only alliteration, *cynghanedd sain*, which uses internal rhyme as well as alliteration, and *cynghanedd lusg*, which uses only internal rhyme :

---

[1] In the abbreviated and simplified exposition that follows I have depended heavily upon John Morris-Jones, *Cerdd Dafod* (Oxford, 1925), chap. iv.

I. *Cynghanedd gytsain*

1. The most difficult form of *cynghanedd* is *cynghanedd groes*, in which the consonantal pattern of the first half-line must be matched exactly by the pattern of the second half. This may take one of three forms :

(*a*) Each half-line ends on an accented syllable ; the consonants *before* the accents must correspond, e.g.

> Mae'n llai'r gwrid ‖ mewn llawer grudd.

(*b*) Each half-line ends on an unaccented syllable ; there must be complete correspondence of the consonants before the accents, *and* of any consonants *between* the accented and the unaccented vowels that conclude each half-line, e.g.

> Ag i hengleirch ‖ gwahanglaf.

(*c*) The first half-line ends on an accented syllable, the second on an unaccented ; there must be complete correspondence of the consonants before the accents, and any consonants after the accented vowel that ends the first half must be matched by the consonants between the accented vowel and the unaccented in the second half, e.g.

> Yr haul wen ‖ a'r haelioni.

2. Another form of purely alliterative *cynghanedd* is *cynghanedd draws* : this is similar to *cynghanedd groes*, but unalliterated consonants begin the second half-line before the consonants of the first half are matched, e.g.

> A braich hir ‖ fal wybr uwch haul.

The three forms of *cynghanedd draws* follow the same rules as those given above for *cynghanedd groes*.

3. The third form of purely alliterative *cynghanedd* is *cynghanedd groes o gyswllt*, in which the matching of consonants is begun *before* the pause at mid-line ; there are again three forms, depending on the placing of the accents, e.g.

> Rufain dwg eirf ‖ yn dy gylch.
> Gloyw ar fwnwgl ‖ ir feinwyn.
> Serch a rois ‖ ar chwaer Esyllt..

II. *Cynghanedd sain*

In the *cynghanedd* that combines internal rhyme with alliteration, the line is divided into three parts : the first and second parts of the line rhyme, and the second internal rhyme is linked to the third part of the line by either *cynghanedd groes* or *cynghanedd draws*. There are four forms of *cynghanedd sain*, according to the accentuation of the second and third parts :

1. The second internal rhyme and the end-rhyme are both accented, e.g.

Nid gwahodd glwth ‖ i fwth ‖ fýdd.

2. The second internal rhyme and the end-rhyme are both unaccented, e.g.

Gwell bedd ‖ a górwĕdd ‖ gwírion.
Defyrn ‖ méddgy̆rn ‖ gormóddgăs.

The first example here uses *cynghanedd groes* to link the third part ; the second uses *cynghanedd draws*.

3. The second internal rhyme is accented, the end-rhyme unaccented, e.g.

Pob glân ‖ i lán ‖ alúniwy̆d.

4. The second internal rhyme is unaccented, the end-rhyme accented ; only the consonants before the accented vowel of the second rhyme must be matched in the third part, e.g.

Aeth dy wedd, ‖ Gwýnedd ‖ a'i gŵýr.

III. *Cynghanedd lusg*

This is the simplest form of *cynghanedd*, in which a syllable in the first half-line rhymes with the accented penultimate syllable of the second half, e.g.

Heddiw mewn pridd yn ddiddim.

Of the three types of *cynghanedd*, the third is the easiest to produce in English : my translation of the line given as an example of *cynghanedd lusg* shows this, 'Today in earth he's worthless.' *Cynghanedd sain* is more difficult, and *cynghanedd gytsain* nearly impossible, at least for a sequence of lines that make sense. If the bards used *cynghanedd* only occasionally, one might try to reproduce it, or feel that not too much was lost without it ; but while the fourteenth-century bards felt free to use it heavily or sparingly, its use became compulsory in the following century. I doubt that there is any solution to the problem thus posed for the translator : the achievement of an original poem, let alone a translation, with *cynghanedd* in each line goes against the grain of the English language ; certainly it demands a technical dexterity I do not possess. I have in general employed alliteration and internal rhyme as fully as possible, hoping to give a kind of 'flavour' of the Welsh originals, and that I have not destroyed all their 'sweetness and harmony', even though much is lost.

Because of the abundance of Welsh personal and place names in the book, and the impossibility of satisfactory transliteration, I have provided a brief guide to the pronunciation of Welsh. I have generally preferred to use the Welsh names and spellings for persons and places, sometimes for metrical convenience (Môn for Anglesey), chiefly for connotation (Lleucu Llwyd is not the same girl if the bard is made to address her as Lucy Gray).

The texts on which I have based the translations are cited in the notes. In deciding on titles, division into sections, and punctuation, I have sometimes followed the standard editions, sometimes my own bent.

The reader who wishes a fuller treatment of this poetry than I have been able to give in this introduction, and who wishes to see it in the context of Welsh literary history, should consult Dr. Parry's book previously cited, to which I am much indebted. Both H. Idris Bell's *The Development of Welsh Poetry* (Oxford, 1936) and Gwyn Williams's *An Introduction to Welsh Poetry* (London, 1953), which first roused my own interest in these lyrics, can be recommended. Other translations of some of the poems, on principles different from mine, can be found in *A Book of Wales* (London, 1953), edited by D. M. and E. M. Lloyd, and in Gwyn Williams's *The Rent that's Due to Love* (London, 1950) and *The Burning*

Tree (London, 1956) : all three contain translations of poems from the earlier medieval period. The fullest attempt to bring the poems of the *cywyddwyr* into English prior to this has been made by H. Idris and David Bell in their *Dafydd ap Gwilym : Fifty Poems* (London, 1942), and in their translations of poems by other bards in *Transactions of the Honourable Society of Cymmrodorion* for 1940 and 1942. Kenneth Jackson has provided prose versions of some of these lyrics in *A Celtic Miscellany* (London, 1951). Essays on both the history and the literature of the period can be found in the two volumes edited by A. J. Roderick, *Wales Through the Ages* (Llandybie, 1959, 1960).

I must thank the administration of Marymount Manhattan College for their continued trust and encouragement, and for the Fathers' Association Research Grant and the Faculty Fellowship that have made this work possible.

I am particularly grateful to the American Philosophical Society for the grant from the Penrose Fund which enabled me to spend four months in Wales completing the book.

For the use of their facilities during those months I wish to thank The National Library of Wales and the University College of Wales, Aberystwyth.

I am deeply indebted for their advice and assistance to Dr. Robert Meyer of Catholic University, and to Dr. Thomas Parry, Professor Thomas Jones, and Mr. Garfield Hughes of the University College of Wales, Aberystwyth.

Mr. D. J. Bowen, of the latter, has been most generous with his time and knowledge, and for such accuracy as these translations possess the credit is largely his. Any errors that remain are, of course, my responsibility.

To be a poet's friend is to become a poet's audience. My colleague, Mr. Robert K. Windbiel, has been a patient listener throughout my years of work on these poems, and I owe much to his judgment, far more to his faith in my ability.

My deepest debt no word or gesture, public or private, can express. Yet I dedicate this book to my wife.

Aberystwyth, Wales, May 1963

THE PRONUNCIATION OF WELSH

The Welsh alphabet uses 28 letters : a, b, c, ch, d, dd, e, f, ff, g, ng, h, i, l, ll, m, n, o, p, ph, r, rh, s, t, th, u, w, y.

In general, the consonants represent the same sound-values as in English spelling, with these exceptions :

c : always the sound it stands for in 'cat', never the sound in 'cease'.

ch : as in the Scottish word 'loch'.

dd : the sound represented by 'th' in 'breathe' ; Welsh uses its 'th' only for the sound in 'breath'.

f : as in 'of'.

ff : as in 'off'.

g : always the sound in 'give', never the sound in 'germ'.

ll : there is no equivalent sound in English ; the usual advice is to pronounce 'tl' rapidly as if it were a single sound, or to put the tip of the tongue on the roof of the mouth and hiss.

ph : as in 'physic'.

r : the sound is always trilled.

rh : the trilled 'r' followed by aspiration.

s : always the sound in 'sea', never the sound in 'does'. 'Si' is used for the sound represented in English spelling by 'sh' ; English 'shop' becomes Welsh 'siop'.

Welsh letters stand always for pure vowel-sounds, never as in English spelling for diphthongs. The vowels can be long or short ; a circumflex accent is sometimes used to distinguish the long vowel.

a : the vowel-sounds in 'father' and (American) 'hot'.

e : the vowel-sounds in 'pale' and 'pet'.

i : the vowel-sounds in 'green' and 'grin'. The letter is also used for the consonantal sound represented in English spelling by 'y' ; English 'yard' becomes Welsh 'iard'.

21

o : the vowel-sounds in 'roll' and (British) 'hot'.

u : pronounced like the Welsh 'i'. Never used as in English spelling for such sounds as 'oo' and 'uh'.

w : the vowel-sounds in 'tool' and 'took'. English 'fool' becomes Welsh 'ffŵl'. The letter is also used consonantally as in English, 'dwelling', 'Gwen'.

y : In most monosyllables and in final syllables it is pronounced like the Welsh 'i'. In other syllables it stands for the vowel-sound in 'up', and this is also its sound in a few monosyllables like 'y' and 'yr'.

The following diphthongs are used in Welsh ; the chief vowel comes first :

ae, ai, au : the diphthong sound in 'write'.

ei, eu, ey : 'uh-ee'.

aw : the diphthong sound in 'prowl'.

ew : the short Welsh 'e' followed by 'oo'.

iw, yw : 'ee-oo'.

wy : 'oo-ee'.

oe, oi, ou : the sound in 'oil'.

The accent in Welsh is placed, with few exceptions, on the next to the last syllable : Mórfudd, Llanbádarn.

Dafydd ap Gwilym

THE SEAGULL

Fair gull on the warm tide-flow,
The hue of snow or pale moon,
Unblemished is your beauty,
Sea's gauntlet, splinter of sun.
Light you are on a sea-swell,
Fishfeeder, stately and swift.
Near you'd go, next the anchor,
Sea lily, we're hand-in-hand,
Paper's twin, glossy-textured,
Nun topping the rising tide.

Go praising a far-famed girl
To curve of fort and castle.
Keep a close lookout, seagull,
For an Eigr on the white fort.
Speak my neatly woven words :
Go to her, bid her choose me.
If she's alone, then greet her ;
Be deft with the dainty girl
To win her : say I shall die,
This well-bred lad, without her.

I love her, source of all bliss.
Ah men, neither Taliesin
Nor free-flattering Merlin
Ever loved a lovelier :
Strife-stirring copper-framed face,
Proud beauty, far too proper.

Gull, if you glimpse the fairest
Maiden's cheek in Christendom,
Should I win no sweet greeting,
Ah God, the girl dooms me dead.

IN A TAVERN

I came to a choice city,
Behind me my handsome squire.
High living, a festive place,
I found, swaggering youngster,
A decent enough public
Lodging, and I ordered wine.

I spied a slim fair maiden
In the house, my pretty dear,
Set wholly, hue of sunrise,
My heart on my slender sweet.
I bought roast, not for boasting,
And costly wine for us two.
Playing the game young men love,
I called her, sweet girl, over.
I whispered, bold, attentive,
That's for sure, two magic words :
I made, love was not idle,
A compact to come to her
When the others had fallen
Fast asleep ; dark-browed was she.

After all were, sad journey,
Asleep but the girl and me,
Painstakingly I sought for
The girl's bed ; and then came grief.
I had, loud it resounded,
A hard fall, no skill at all ;
I could rise, wicked it was,
More clumsily than quickly.
I bumped, by jumping badly,
My shin, and how my leg hurt,
Against, an ostler left it,
The side of a noisy stool.

In coming, penitent tale,
Above, the Welsh girl loved me,
I struck, great lust is evil,
The place was, not one free step,
A trap where blows were traded,
My head on a table top
Where there lay a loose basin
And a booming pan of bronze.
From the table fell, wild room,
All it held and both trestles,
Raising clamour from the pan
After me, far-flung racket,
And clanging, I was helpless,
From the basin, and dogs barked.

Next the thick walls there lay in
A stinking bed three Saxons
Bothered about their bundles,
Hickin and Jenkin and Jack.
Whispered the filthy-mouthed lad,
Angry speech, to the others :
'A Welshman's, din to dupe us,
Stalking here treacherously ;
He'll steal, if we allow it ;
Take heed, be on your guard.'

Then rose a crowd of ostlers
Thronging, a terrible tale.
Frowning they were around me,
Searching for my hiding place,
And me, with ugly bruises,
Keeping quiet in the dark.
I prayed, in no bold fashion,
Hidden, like a timid girl,
And by prayer's wondrous might,
And by the grace of Jesus,

I gained, a sleepless tangle,
Unrequited, my own bed.
I escaped, the saints were kind :
Of God I ask forgiveness.

A CELEBRATION OF SUMMER

Summer, parent of impulse,
Begetter of close-knit boughs,
Warden, lord of wooded slopes,
Tower to all, hills' tiler,
You're the cauldron, wondrous tale,
Of Annwn, life's renewal,
It's you are, source of singing,
The home of each springing shoot,
Balm of growth, burgeoning throng,
And chrism of crossing branches.

Your hand, by the Lord we love,
Knows how to make trees flourish.
Essence of earth's four corners,
By your grace wondrously grow
Birds and the fair land's harvest
And the swarms that soar aloft,
Moorland meadows' bright-tipped hay,
Strong flocks and wild bees swarming.
You foster, highways' prophet,
Earth's burden, green-laden garths.
You make my bower blossom,
Building a fine web of leaves.
And wretched it is always
Near August, by night or day,
Knowing by the slow dwindling,
Golden store, that you must go.

Tell me, summer, this does harm,
I have the art to ask you,
What region, what countryside,
What land you seek, by Peter.
'Hush, bard of praise, your smooth song,
Hush, strong boast so enchanting.
My fate it is, mighty feat,
As a prince,' sang the sunshine,
'To come three months to nourish
Foodstuff for the multitude ;
And when roof and growing leaves
Wither, and woven branches,
To shun the winds of winter
Deep down to Annwn I go.'

The blessings of the world's bards
And their good words go with you.
Farewell, king of fair weather,
Farewell, our ruler and lord,
Farewell, the fledgling cuckoos,
Farewell, balmy banks in June,
Farewell, sun high above us
And the broad sky, round white ball.
You'll not be, king of legions,
So high, crest of drifting cloud,
Till come, fair hills unhidden,
Summer once more and sweet slopes.

IFOR HAEL

Ifor, fair stewardship's gold
Is mine, delightful nurture.
I too, bountiful ruler,
Am your steward, you're much blessed.

It's a grand, you are mindful,
Store for me, you're a fine man.
I paid you the tongue's sweet praise,
You paid me bright dark bragget.
You gave coin, friendly gesture,
I name you 'The Generous'.
Strong blade, no blades restrain you,
Comrade and bondsman of bards.
Mighty prince, mighty lineage,
Captive of bards, wealthy lord.
You're the bravest, fiercest man
To follow, a strong fellow.
Fine and proud's your pedigree ;
God knows, you're twice as docile
To your bard, no dishonour,
Warlord, as this hand to that.

I leave my land, noble branch,
With your praise, I come, Ifor.
From my speech comes the image,
No base word, of what you are.
From my mouth, lord of many,
Multitudes will sing your praise.
As far as man may journey,
As the summer sun can roam,
As far as the wheat is sown,
As far as fair dew moistens,
As far as a clear eye sees,
It's keen, far as ear's hearing,
As far as Welsh is spoken,
And as far as fine seeds grow,
Handsome, courteous Ifor,
Long sword, your praise will be sown.

THE GIRLS OF LLANBADARN

Passion doubles me over,
Plague take all the parish girls !
Because, frustrated trysting,
I've had not a single one.
No lovely longed-for virgin,
Not a wench nor witch nor wife.

What's the hindrance, what mischief,
What flaw, that I'm not desired ?
What harm if a slim-browed girl
Has me in a dark forest ?
No shame for her to see me
Lying in a bed of leaves.
Not a time I wasn't loving,
Never was there such a spell
Except for men like Garwy,
One or two each single day,
And for all that, no nearer
To finding a friendly one.

No Sunday in Llanbadarn
I was not, as some will swear,
Facing a dainty maiden,
The nape of my neck to God.
And when I've long been staring
Over my plume at the pews,
Says one maiden, clear and bright,
To her shrewd, pretty neighbour :
'That lad, palefaced as a flirt,
Wearing his sister's tresses,
Adulterous the slanting
Glances of his eye : he's *bad* !'
'Do you think he's showing off ?'
Says the one who is next her,

'He'll never have an answer :
To the devil, foolish thing !'

Cruel the fine girl's cursing,
Small pay for a love-dazed man.
I am forced to call a halt
To my ways, to these nightmares.
I'm compelled to leave like one
Who's a hermit, an outlaw.
Too much looking, strange lesson,
Behind me, a feeble sight,
Leaves me, lover of strong song,
Head bowed with no companion.

THE OWL

A sorry creature's the foul
Sad owl who won't be quiet.
She permits me no *pater*,
She's not still while stars are out.
Not for me, O forbidden,
A doze or a peaceful sleep.
House humping, amid the bats,
Its back to snow and drizzle.

In my ears, small charm for me,
Each night, memory's pennies,
When I close, public nuisance,
My eyes, the realms of honour,
This wakes me, I have not slept,
The owl's cry and her singing,
Her constant screech and laughter,
And the false notes from her throat.
From then, that's the way I live,
Till dawning, mournful passion,
She keeps singing, mournful cry,

'Hoo-thee-hoo,' lively longing.
Full force, by Saint Anne's grandson,
She stirs up the curs of night.

She's a slut, two tuneless cries,
Thick head, persistent crying,
Broad forehead, berry-bellied,
Staring old mouse-hunting hag.
Stubborn, vile, lacking colour,
Dry her voice, her colour tin,
Loud gabble in the south wood,
O that song, roebuck's copses,
And her face, a meek maiden's,
And her shape, a ghostly bird.
Every bird, filthy outlaw,
Beats her ; how strange she still lives.

More talkative in woodlands
By night than the nightingale,
By day she'll not stick, strict rule,
Her head from a tree's hollow.
Piercing wail, well I know her,
She is Gwyn ap Nudd's own bird.
Fool owl who croons to robbers,
Cursed be her tongue and her tune !

I have a song for scaring
The owl from my neighbourhood :
I'll set, waiting for winter,
A blaze by each ivied tree.

THE GIRL OF EITHINFYNYDD

The girl of Eithinfynydd,
My sweet soul, who wants no tryst,
Slender brows, gentle glances,

Fine gold hair, fleeting frown,
My blessing until bleak death,
My young and tender goddess,
My glowing, golden mirror,
She's my fate, my girl of gold,
My prize in the hill's shelter,
My love for her grows and grows.

My jewel, fine-haired maiden,
My dear's not had on the hill.
She'll not seek the wooded slope,
Nor love her love, nor frolic.
Morfudd's not for fun and games,
She's not won, she loves Mary,
Loves the saints, splendid power,
Loves God : she's no faith in me.

The fair one, she's capricious,
Does not know how odd she is.
She's known no adultery,
She craved not me, nor any.
I would not wish, my darling,
To live, lacking my fine girl.
From this pain that's upon me,
Gentle Morfudd, I shall die.

A STUBBORN GIRL

As I was walking over
A mountain, men of Christ's creed,
Like a farmer, my gay cloak
Round me, in summer yearning,
Look : a limb of a maiden's
Waiting for me on the moor.
I greeted her, gentle swan,

Sweetly, dear discreet maiden.
She gave her bard an answer,
An answer, I thought, of love.

Arm in arm, like May's daughters,
The cold girl would not consent.
I was wild for the maiden,
She was not wild to be kissed.
When I praise her sparkling eyes,
She praises handsome poets.
I begged her, before war came,
To have me : she's my heaven.

'You'll not, lad of the hillside,
Be answered ; I'm still not sure.
We'll to Llanbadarn Sunday
Or the tavern, artful man ;
And there in the green woodland
Or heaven we'll have a tryst.
I wish none, for fear of scorn,
To know I'm in the birch-grove.'

'Your love deems me a coward,
Your wooer's a daring man.
Do not shun me, splendid thatch,
Fearing some woman's clatter.
I know of a greenwood nook
Never known by another ;
No jealous man will know it
While the trees and twigs stay veiled.
Yield to my pleading, maiden,
Protectress, thief of the grove.'

The wayward girl did not keep
To her word, cuckoo's cousin.
Foolish the pledge that cheered me,
Pledge of wine, such is her tryst.

THE RATTLE BAG

As I lay, fullness of praise,
On a summer day under
Trees between field and mountain
Awaiting my soft-voiced girl,
She came, there's no denying,
Where she vowed, a very moon.
Together we sat, fine theme,
The girl and I, debating,
Trading, while I had the right,
Words with the splendid maiden.

And so we were, she was shy,
Learning to love each other,
Concealing sin, winning mead,
An hour lying together,
And then, cold comfort, it came,
A blare, a bloody nuisance,
A sack's bottom's foul seething
From an imp in shepherd's shape,
Who had, public enemy,
A harsh-horned sag-cheeked rattle.
He played, cramped yellow belly,
This bag, curse its scabby leg.
So before satisfaction
The sweet girl panicked : poor me !
When she heard, feeble-hearted,
The stones whir, she would not stay.

By Christ, no Christian country,
Cold harsh tune, has heard the like.
Noisy pouch perched on a pole,
Bell of pebbles and gravel,
Saxon rocks making music
Quaking in a bullock's skin,

Crib of three thousand beetles,
Commotion's cauldron, black bag,
Field-keeper, comrade of straw,
Black-skinned, pregnant with splinters,
Noise that's an old buck's loathing,
Devil's bell, stake in its crotch,
Scarred pebble-bearing belly,
May it be sliced into thongs.
May the churl be struck frigid,
Amen, who scared off my girl.

GILDING THE LILY

Some of the country maidens,
For the fair, delightful day,
With pearls and a bright ruby
Deck their pretty golden brows,
Don red, a girl's best setting,
And green — poor men who've no girls !
Not an arm, heavy burden,
Or neck of a slim-browed girl
Uncircled, hawks of summer,
With beads, a fabulous life.

Must the sun, a costly trip,
Leave heaven for more colour ?
No more need my fair girl place
A frontlet on her forehead,
Nor gaze into yonder glass :
Her looks are very lovely.

The yew-bow may be unsound,
Two halves it's hardly reckoned :
For the market, deathless goods,
Its back is brightly gilded ;

At a high price it's selling,
This bow, believe me it's true.
No one thinks, a good proverb,
A fair thing's frail or a fraud.

Mary ! is the white wall worse
Under lime, a fine coating,
Than if, false values of man,
A pound were paid the painter
To adorn, pretty purpose,
A bare wall with brilliant gold,
And still more glowing colours,
And the shapes of splendid shields?

Kept from, my flesh, where I'd come,
Hue of stars, I am hurting.
You, your dear one's destroyer,
White-toothed mite worthy of praise,
In fine white shift are fairer
Than a countess gowned in gold.

UNDER THE EAVES

Locked was the door of the house :
I am ill, my dear, hear me.
Come into view, fair figure,
For God's sake, make yourself seen.
Why should a liar triumph ?
By Mary, it drives one mad.
Love-confounded, I pounded
Three strong strokes that broke the locked
Latch : it was quite a noise, no ?
Did you hear ? A bell's clangour.

Morfudd, my chaste-minded love,
Nurse of deceit's dominion,
I lie a wall's breadth away
From you : I must shout, dearest.
Have pity on sleepless pain,
Dark the night, love-deceiver.
Notice my sad condition :
O God, what weather tonight !
Often the eaves spill water
On my means of love, my flesh ;
No more rain, love-pained am I,
Than snow, and me below it.
Uncosy is this quaking ;
Never had man's flesh more pain
Than I have had from longing :
By God, there's no viler bed.
There never in Caernarvon
Was a jail worse than this road.
I'd not be nightlong out here,
I would not groan, but for you ;
Nor come to suffer, be sure,
Nightly, unless I loved you ;
Nor stay under snow and rain,
Except for you, one minute ;
Nor renounce, mine the anguish,
All the world were there no you.

Here am I, in cold weather ;
Lucky you, you're in the house.
My pure soul is within there,
And here outside is my ghost.
A listener would be doubtful
That I, my treasure, will live.
My thoughts are not of leaving,
It was madness drove me here.
I entered an agreement :
I am here — and where are you ?

THE GREY FRIAR

A shame the much-praised maiden
Does not know, the grove's her court,
The speech of the Grey Friar
About her this very day.

I visited the friar
To confess a sin of mine,
Admitted to him, truly,
That I was a kind of bard,
And that I had loved always
A pale-faced, dark-browed maiden,
And my slayer allowed me
No queenly kindness, no prize,
Nothing but drawn-out loving,
Longing deeply for her love,
Bearing her praise throughout Wales,
And lacking her despite that,
And yearning to feel her in
Bed between me and the wall.

Said the friar to me then,
'I could give you good counsel,
If you've loved one white as foam,
Hue of paper, long till now.
Lessen the pain that's coming,
To cease is good for your soul,
Silencing your cywyddau,
Acquaint yourself with *paters*.
Not for cywydd or englyn
Has the Lord redeemed man's soul.
There's naught in your songs, you bards,
But nonsense and vain noises,
Inciting men and women
To sin and unfaithfulness.

No good's sensual praise that
Draws the soul to the devil.'

Then I answered the friar
For each word he had spoken :
'The Lord is not as cruel
As old men say that He is.
He'll not let a dear soul go
For loving wife or maiden.
Three things are loved through the world :
Woman, health, and fair weather.

'A girl's the fairest blossom
In heaven save God himself.
From woman was each man born
Of all folk, three excepted.
And therefore it's no wonder
We love maidens and matrons.
Gladness was bred in heaven,
The whole of sadness in hell.

'It's song that makes merrier
Old and young, frail and lusty.
My need to fashion verses
Is strong as your need to preach,
My roving as a bard is
As proper as your begging.
Are not sequences and hymns
Made up of odes and englyns ?
The prophet David's psalms are
Cywyddau to holy God.

'Not on one meat and morsel
Does the Lord sustain mankind.
A time was given for food,
And a time for devotion,

D

A time for preaching sermons,
A time for making merry.
Song is sung at each banquet
To give delight to maidens,
Pater in church to ask for
The country of Paradise.

'True is Ystudfach's saying
In carousing with his bards :
"A happy face, a full house ;
A sad face, evil dwells there."
Though some may love saintliness,
Others love entertainment.
Few men know a sweet cywydd,
And all men know their *pater*,
And so, censorious friar,
Song is not the greatest sin.

'When it's as good for all men
To hear a harp-sung *pater*
As for the girls of Gwynedd
To hear a lusty cywydd,
I'll sing, I swear by this hand,
The *pater* without ceasing.
Till then, shame on Dafydd if
He sings aught save a cywydd.'

THE HOLLY GROVE

Holly grove fully laden,
Smiling fort, with coral fruit,
Fair choir by man unravaged,
Snug-roofed close, a house for two,
Keep where a girl can kiss me,
Pointed beaks, spur-bearing leaves.

I'm a man who strolls near slopes
Beneath trees, fine-haired branches ;
Grace-tended, splendid structure,
I've strolled through dales, trees, and leaves.
Who in winter ever found
The month of May's green livery ?
Thought to hold, I found today
A hillside grove of holly.
Love's cradle, leaves thick-crowded,
May's own livery, this was mine,
Woodland cradle, organ loft,
Fine palace on green pillars,
Song's pantry above the snows,
Penthouse, by God's hand painted.

God can make a gift that's twice
As good as lavish Robert's.
Generous Hywel Fychan,
Solemn song, skilfully shaped,
Praised, no villein, a woodland
Angel in a lovely bed.
Beautiful wayside branches,
Thick stubbled servant, green cloaked,
Home of birds from Paradise,
Dome of leaves, green and comely,
No old hut, rain-thirsty room,
Snug will be nights beneath it.
The leaves will scarcely wither
On the holly tipped with steel.
Old buck or goat from Severn
Will not chew his fill of this.
Iron muzzle, when long nights
Bring frost to moor and valley,
No share of the grove is lost,
Despite cold spring-wind crying,
Camlet of loyal green leaves
Woven on hillside branches.

THE COWARD

'Languid girl, lovely daybreak,
Dark brows, decked with gold and gems,
Reckon, Eigr, with awgrim stones,
Beneath green leaves, what's due me,
A strict clear-voiced accounting,
Lovely gem, for how I've sung
Your bright hue, glowing language,
And your form, bright gossamer.'

'I've long pardoned you, Dafydd,
Love's turned witless, you're to blame,
For being, fear's familiar,
A coward, your rightful name.
None shall have me, Lord help me,
You're fearful, man, but the brave.'

'Cowled in fine hair, fine-spun web,
You wrong me, sweet-voiced maiden.
Though well-bred, tender-hearted,
Timid in war, breast too bared,
Not timid, where green leaves grow,
Am I in Ovid's business.

'And also (Eigr's own image)
Consider (is your smooth brow),
Throbbing pain, no good's the love
Of a brave lad, sad torment,
For a warrior, crude fellow,
Is likely to be a boor.
Savage he'll be and untamed,
Loving war and cold weather.
Should he hear, hot for conquest,
Of a French or Scottish war,
A brave venture, there he'll go
To have his name enlisted.

Should he, let's suppose, escape
From there, with the French bridled,
Scarred he'll be, archers crush him,
And vicious, my shining girl.
He has more love for his lance
And sword, it's grief to trust him,
His plain shield, and steel armour,
And horse, than for a fair girl.
He'll not screen you from slander,
He'll not court but capture you.

'Now I, with lively language,
Were you mine, bright gossamer,
I know how, I'd weave strict song,
Listen, girl, to conceal you.
If I had, fast in my grasp,
Girl fair as Deifi, two kingdoms,
Sun's hue, I'd not, despite them,
Day's light, leave your bright abode.'

THE DREAM

As I lay, skilled in hiding,
Sleeping in a secret place,
I saw as day was breaking
A dream on the brow of dawn.
I saw that I was walking,
My pack of hounds at my side,
Down a slope to a forest,
Fine place, no surly churl's home.
I loosed without delaying,
I thought, my dogs to the woods.

I heard cries, angry voices,
Many sounds, pursuing hounds.

A white hind above the glades
I saw, I loved the quarry,
And the pack of hounds trailing
On her track, in sure pursuit,
Across a wooded hillcrest,
Across two ridges and peaks,
And back across the summits
On the same course as the deer,
And she came to me, turned tame,
And I enraged, for refuge.
Bare nostrils, I awakened,
Sharp-set, I was in the hut.

Luckily, when it was day,
I found a kind old woman.
I told my story to her,
What I saw, the night's omen :
'By God, wise woman, if you
Have skill to solve this vision,
I'll compare, how I'm wounded,
None with you.   I'm in despair.'

'A good thing, desperate man,
Is your dream, if you're manly.
The dogs you saw so clearly
By your side, if rightly read,
Good trackers at their trailing,
Are your messengers of love.
And the white hind, the princess
You loved, hue of sunlit foam,
This is certain, she will come
To your keeping, and God keep you.'

MORFUDD'S ARMS

Her figure, formed like Enid's,
And gold locks set me aflame.

Bared brow, a lily petal,
Queenly and gentle her hand,
A graceful girl, well-mannered
And womanly, none's her peer.
Her arms compelled by longing
Came round my neck at the tryst,
A thing that seldom happened,
Holding me fast with her lips.
Lovely wine-bred form's weak bard,
I then became her captive.

Imprudently, now there is,
A gift it was, God's witness,
Love's knot, though I conceal it,
Between us, surely, I'm bound.
Gracious, glowing, snowdrift arms
Of Morfudd, cheeks of sunlight,
Held me, not hard if she's bold,
Face to face in the arbour.
Well did she, soft and slender,
Enclose me with loving arms,
Fast in a knot of pure love
The wrists of my true sweetheart.
Mine, for my zealous journey,
Bold collar of secret love.

Bard's smooth yoke, lovely jewel,
No burden were her bright arms.
Beneath her celebrant's ear
A collar, unresisted,
Chalk-coloured, a snow circle,
Fine gift to deck a man's neck,
The girl gave, one that's supple,
Round her bard's throat, slender gem.
Splendid sight in the bracken,
A Tegau choking a man.
And then in a faster clasp,

Hue of gold, O that necklace !
I was readily spellbound ;
Long live the bewitching girl
Who holds me, fine arrangement,
Caressing me like a nurse.

Unkind are those who'd scorn me,
Sun's likeness, within her arms :
Fearless, no coward, bold browed
And black am I, and reckless,
And my faithful girl's two arms
Round me — is mead for drinking ?
Drunk I was, I endured it,
Drunk with a strong slender girl.
My joy without vexation,
The white necklace her arms made :
Well cherished in her embrace,
This once they were my collar.

MORFUDD'S OATH

Better a hurt, fancied wrong,
Than surly, boorish sulking.
Good to her man shall Morfudd
Be at last, radiant as snow.

Her oath, luminous Luned,
She graciously gave to me,
Upon her hand, ring-laden,
And her arm and her whole heart,
To love me, mankind's monarch,
If ape loves his foster-son.
Fine oath, if it's not cancelled,
Blessed will I be, if it's true.
I never, secret pleasure,
Had a reward from the first

To match having such kindness,
If this is an honest gift.
No jewel, foolish notion,
Nor glen's birches, nor false gem,
But Mary's own Son's goldcraft
With His bare hand by God's light,
Psalm of the Lord, has sealed it
With His blessing and His grace :
Enough it was and will be
To bind us to each other,
And long and deep in the flames
Will stay the one who breaks it.

And I too gave my darling,
To that graceful, shapely girl,
A firm oath, not a fragile,
On her hand, hue of the sun,
As she gave me, free and strong,
In water, by name, Dafydd,
Love's mighty pain, the Lord's love,
To love her, drifted snowfall.

An honest oath was given,
Well I know it, made by God.
My sweetheart with her fair hand
Gave this handful, God bless it,
A kind, perfect, binding oath,
True fidelity's virtue,
Oath to God with her right hand,
No empty oath, I know it,
Sprightly sprig, form of Indeg,
A good oath on her fair hand.
Love's book will be in her hand,
Ruler, sole lord of summer.
Confirmed in the cold water
Was the oath Morfudd Llwyd gave.

THE WAVE

Curly-topped loud-crying wave,
Bar not, fair hopes, my passage
To that shore, where waits my reward,
Make no delay, no hindrance.
Let me, for God's sake, great lord,
Surging water, cross Dyfi.
Turn, home of three-hundred nets,
I'm your bard, crest of water.

Whose lips have sung as often
Praise of your masterful roar,
Comrade of sail, sea's jewel,
Crosier of ocean, as mine ?
No great gale from the planets,
No swift rush between steep banks,
Nor keen conflict, nor scourge-stick,
Nor shoulder of soldier or steed
I've not compared, sore my pain,
Pulsing wave, to your power.
Not a harp, not an organ,
Not a flawless singing voice
I've not judged by the force of,
Fresh torrent, your full-toned sound.
I'll not speak one more word of
My love, fatal snare like Nyf,
Without calling her brightness
And her fair face like your stream.

See, then, you do not thwart me,
Clear-rippling bright amazon,
From going, my dear's my judge,
Through birches near Llanbadarn
To her who made, prolific,
Dear maiden, me live once more.
My mind is sorely straitened,

Lady, rider of the sea.
You bar me from my region ;
Bridle the stream with your snout.

If you knew, pale-mantled wave,
Fair go-between of fishes,
How she'll scold if I delay !
You are the far shore's mantle :
Though come for one like Indeg
As far as your breast, fair wave,
No foe's attack will kill me ;
If you keep me from the girl,
Love's fevers will be my death :
Bar me not from my Morfudd.

THE MASS OF THE GROVE

In a pleasant place today,
Mantled by fine green hazel,
I listened at day's dawning
To a skilful speckled thrush
Singing a polished stanza,
Smooth lessons and prophecies.
The essence of discretion,
Love's messenger journeyed long,
Coming from fair Carmarthen
At my golden girl's command,
Wordy, needing no password,
To this spot, to Nentyrch brook.
Morfudd it was who sent him,
This melodious child of May.

About him there were hangings,
Blossoms of May's precious boughs,
His chasuble (they seemed like)

Of the wind's (green mantles) wings.
All gold, by God almighty,
Was the altar's canopy.
I heard in glowing language
A long, no faltering, chant,
No stumble or mumble, that
Read gospel to the parish.
On a hill of ashtrees there
He raised a leafy wafer,
And a nightingale near by,
Beautiful, slim, sweet-spoken,
The brook's songstress, rang sanctus
To the welkin, clear her call.
The offering was lofted
To heaven above the grove,
Worship to God our Father,
A chalice of bliss and love.

Such liturgy contents me,
Bred of birches in fair woods.

A GARLAND OF PEACOCK FEATHERS

At daybreak, dawn of desire,
I trysted with my sweetheart,
Both bent on love, true passion,
In woodland aisle weaving song.
I asked my love, old as I,
To twine twigs from the saplings,
Pretty horns, a gay chaplet,
A garland for me, bright green.
'Fashion love's faultless circle,'
And the girl answered her bard :

'Pure your voice, skilful singing,
Know you not, complaint of pain,

It's a poor thing, no pleasure,
To strip birches till they die.
The birches have, gentle trees,
No leaves fit for the taking.
I'll not weave twigs together,
It's wrong to rob groves of leaves.'

She gave me, long it will last,
The gift I'll guard for ever,
Fine as gold cloth, a garland
Of peacock plumes for my head,
Superb chaplet, bright linen,
Pretty blossoms of gay plumes,
Lovely web of gleaming twigs,
Butterflies, leafy jewels.
Kingly work, it was comely,
Thickly piled, three-coloured wheels.
Dead men's eyes, glow-worm lanterns,
They are images of moons.
Good to have, never failing,
The mirrors from Virgil's fairs.

Long am I blessed, she gave it,
Garland for her glad-voiced bard.
Praiseworthy deed, her plying
And plaiting feathers and wings.
Slim girl's love-gift for her bard,
God gave it, pretty striping,
All His care, craft of fine gold,
Bright as a gold pavilion.

BETRAYAL

Love on a fickle woman
I lavished, with little gain.
Sorry was I for loving

A false girl, she was my grief,
As I have loved exquisite
Morfudd, day's hue.　No matter.
Morfudd wanted, my darling,
Love no longer.　Sorry turn !

I've spent a share, fool's torment,
Of good song in loving her.
I've spent on worthless minstrels
Fine rings ; downcast am I !
A weir's, that face, strong foaming,
Spent what I had from a gem,
Spent, not like one who's prudent,
Jewels of mine for her sake.
From true passion I fashioned
Poems, and I sang her songs
For bards to Ceri's border,
Hue of fine snow, for her sake.

Her trust in me was vested :
For all this, she was my dear,
I've had, except care's sickness,
No compact, naught in return,
But her lying, deed of wrong,
Snow's hue, beneath another,
To become, worthless labour,
Pregnant, my own little dear.

Whatever, to give me grief,
Has made her, she was spellbound,
Either love it was, leave me,
Evil thought, or violence,
A vile cuckold they call me,
Ah that cry ! by her, foam's hue.
Some place, a sort of symbol,
In my hand, breast sorely tried,
Twigs of, better to burn them,

Green hazel ; I'm not to blame.
Others place, angry purpose,
A willow hat round my head.

Morfudd, none of my choosing,
Not an hour of love, caused this :
God judge truly between us,
That gossamer face and me.

THE WORLD'S BRITTLENESS

Misfortune's mine, angry grief,
Cursed be the one who crossed me !
He it is, terror's timid,
Thieving Eiddig, the land's Jew.
Wealth gave me, no help at hand,
No safeguard, God assessed me.

Festive, well-bred, free-spending,
Well-off and wealthy was I.
I took leave of fine living,
Thought aflame, I'm now in need.
Lavishness, vain love's fashion,
I'm blameless, brought me to naught.

Let none give, straight and handsome,
The world, that traitor, his heart.
Naïve lad, if he gives it,
Brittle world, he'll be deceived.
A charm is wealth, and a foe,
Bitter fray, man's betrayer.
Now it will come, pitch of pride,
Now it will go, for certain,
Like the ebb on the seastrand
After praise and wealth's high tide.

Wise, unvexed, laughs the blackbird
In a green grove, song's sweet room.
Fertile soil's not ploughed for her,
Fresh seed, she needs no ploughing.
And none, little short-legged bird,
With babbling is more lavish.
By God above, she's merry,
Spinning song in woodland grove.
Most merry, lofty-hearted,
Are the minstrels, keeping time.

But I weep, my breast saddened,
Tears' concourse, calling a girl,
And Mary knows, constant praise,
I weep no tears for riches,
Since there's not, lovely concord,
A Welsh-speaking stretch of Wales
Where I'll not win, sweet language,
Fervent lad, wealth for my work,
But of her generation
None under the sun like her.
I was duped of my candle,
Morfudd, bright as day, Llwyd.

LAMENT FOR GRUFFUDD AB ADDA

All's changed by a whitewashed wall,
Proud trees, a crowded orchard,
Where called beneath the apples
The nightingale night and day,
Bird of bright lingering song,
Deep nest, heaven's own fledgling,
From a fair perch golden notes,
From a green bough clear chiming.

Since there came, smoothly turned song,
A fierce archer, quick leaping,
Foully bent on destruction,
With a four-edged birchwood bolt,
Though plentiful, pleasing gift,
Are pears, the trees' fair burden,
Song falters, full of yearning,
The blossoms' bright jewel gone.

Powys, fair land and fruitful,
Fine taverns, sweet drinking-horns,
It was a pleasant orchard
Till blue blade slew this wise lad.
Now it lacks, wretched widow,
Land of hawks, its nightingale.
Poor in bards, song degraded,
Is this land, hated by foes.
If grief must be, these three months,
Ah why was loss no lighter,
When he met, cry of great rage,
A sword's edge where none loved him.

Gruffudd, bird who sang sweetly,
Son of Addaf, blameless man,
All worthy men once called him
A lord of May's lovely boughs,
A cheerful, far-heard organ,
And love's golden nightingale,
A busy melodious bee,
Wise springtime of Gwenwynwyn.

Vile the kinsman who struck him,
Bold wrath, with steel in his hand.
The sword made, cowardly man,
A deep cleft in my brother,
Through the noble hawk's thin hair,
Ah God ! that sword was sharp-edged.

Three-edged the blade, how wretched,
Through the brave man's yellow hair,
Single stroke with the swordblade,
Crude cut through the charming head,
I'm grieved, one stroke, like a goose,
Two halves, was this not boorish ?

Cheeks like a glowing angel,
Tower of gold, the man's gone.

THE SHADOW

Yesterday under fine leaves
I stayed for her, my Helen,
Under a green birch mantle
Safe from the rain, foolish lad.
Then I saw a sort of shape
Standing there, all distorted.
It drew back where it stood and
Faced me, like a friendly man,
And I blessed myself and begged
The saints to ward off evil.

'Tell me, and end your silence,
If you're a man, who you are.'

'I am, desist from questions,
The strange shadow of yourself.
Be still, for your benefit,
That I may speak my message.
I am come, a good custom,
Standing naked by your side,
To reveal, gem of complaints,
What you are, by enchantment.'

'O no, misshapen creature,
I'm not like that, goblin form.
The shape of a hunchbacked goat,
You resemble, queer picture,
More a strange apparition
Than the true form of a man.
Bickering herd in motley,
Legs of a hag on black stilts,
Shepherd of grimy goblins,
Bogey like a bald-pate monk,
Herdsman playing at griors,
Heron feeding in the reeds,
Crane stretching his wings full spread,
Goblin walls, by the cornfield,
A dimwitted palmer's face,
A ragged man's black brother,
Form of a coarsely clad corpse,
Where are you from, old yardpost ?'

'For days, should I accuse you,
I'd stay, what I know's your bane.'

'What fault of mine do you know,
Other, neck of a pitcher,
Than what all men of judgment
Now know ? Devil's shit to you !
I've not disowned my homeland,
Nor struck, I know, a foul blow,
Nor slung a stone at the hens,
Nor said boo to the babies.
I do not twist my talent,
I've not raped a stranger's wife.'

'By my faith, should I tell to
Those who know what I know,
Before the indictment's end,
Faith, you'd be on the gallows.'

'Take care, your snare is cruel,
Not to reveal what you know,
No more, while mine's the secret,
Than lips sewn fast with a stitch.'

DYDDGU

Lord of the spear, worthy sire,
Ieuan, rouser of armies,
Gruffudd's own son, fair wine-fort,
Chieftain, true master of men,
One night I was, high spirits,
At your home, reward be long :
Since then it's not been easy,
Fair colour, for me to sleep.
Your gold was mine, unstinting,
Your bright wine, your merriment,
Your free-flowing mead for bards,
Your dark-topped brew of bragget ;
Your daughter, she would not love,
Fair maid of a stone mansion.

I've not slept, not woven song,
A wink, a prey to fevers.
Holy God, who will ease me ?
Nothing will enter my heart
Except her love that's priceless :
Given all, what need I more ?
She'll not love, fever frets me,
Nor let me sleep, or grow old.

The marvel of Rome's Sages,
My slender dear's wondrous face,
Whiter than snow in springtime ;
Love of her leaves me forlorn.

Under twigs white her forehead,
Black is her hair, she is chaste.
Her hair's blacker, proud forest,
Than blackbird or brooch of jet.
Smooth skin's unblemished whiteness
Darkens her hair, flawless praise.

Her complexion, tranquil day,
Is like, declares her poet,
The kind-hearted girl once loved
By the warrior, I'm wretched,
Peredur, steady staring,
Efrog's son, brave handsome knight,
In his gazing, blaze of light,
At the snow, princely eagle,
Azure sheet near Iseult's grove,
Where the wild hawk left traces
Of killing (none to curb him)
A blackbird, proud maid (from wrong)
There were faithful emblems there
(Is this gift not God's painting ?)
In snow smooth as, heaped snowdrift,
Her forehead, her husband says ;
The wings of the swift blackbird
Like her brow, a spell's on me ;
The bird's blood after snowfall,
Splendour of sun, like her cheeks.

Like this is, gold-cased organ,
Dyddgu, with black glossy hair.
I've played judge, wayward journey,
Let this crowd of critics judge :
Is it worthwhile, my fervour,
To live for my dear one's sake ?

LOVE'S SHAFT

A girl under gleaming gold
I saw, fair as ford foaming,
Every inch of her golden,
Lovely maid the hue of day,
Listening to Noah's psalm
In Saint Deinioel's choir, Bangor.
World's bounty of loveliness,
Woe, Flora's face, betrayal,
Seeing the fair sweet maiden,
Ah the grace ! filled me with pain.

A sevenedged shaft pierced me,
And seven songs of distress.
Poisoned barb, how I'm pining,
Joyful are Môn's jealous men,
None on earth can draw it out,
Deep in the heart it lodges.
No blacksmith shaped its sharpness,
It's made by no honing hand ;
Unknown the hue, fine praises,
And shape of my fatal shaft.

I have grown, life and looks gone,
Frantic for Gwynedd's candle.
Ah God ! how deep the points pierce ;
Bless her ! a face like Mary's.
Pain's firm grip turns me feeble,
Sad creature wasting my cheeks.
The whetted shaft, envenomed,
Hurts keenly, skewer of grief.
An angry Iseult lodged it,
A stake in a battered breast.
Dreadful is its persistence,
Cleaver of my broken breast.
Agony's in love's bradawl,
Treason's twin, thricesharpened shaft.

THE MIST

Thursday, a day to drink on,
Blessed me with, promising gift,
Hope of, I'm lean with yearning,
Learning love in full : I won
A walk in fair-branched greenwoods
With a girl ; she granted a tryst.

There was, by God the Father,
Bless her, not a soul who knew,
Thursday's the day, at dawning,
How brimful I was with joy,
And I went, fine form in view,
To meet the slim young maiden,
When over the long moorland
Came mist the colour of night,
Rain-concealing parchment roll,
Grey ranks to stay my going,
A sieve of metal rusting,
A snare for the black earth's birds,
Blur blocking the narrow path,
The sky's untidy blanket.
Grey cowl discolouring land,
Veil on each hollow valley.
Then are seen the high hurdles,
Mist spilling over the hill,
Thick grey fleece, soft and fragile,
Smoke-coloured, cloaking the field,
Plain of rain thwarting reward,
A heavy shower's armour.

It deceived man, dark-visaged,
Rough cloak of the countryside,
Towers travelling on high,
Tribe of Gwyn, the wind's province.

Its grim cheeks conceal the ground,
Threatens stars with its torches.
Thick-swollen ugly darkness
Blinds the world to cheat a bard,
Wide web of costly cambric
Spread all about like a rope,
Spider-web, stock of French shops,
Gwyn and his tribe's moor headland,
Speckled smoke seen quite often,
Steam rising round trees in May,
Unlovely fog where dogs bark,
Ointment of Annwn's witches.
How strangely it soaks, like dew,
The land's moist blurred habergeon.

The moors by night are simpler
To walk than in daytime's mist ;
The stars come out in the sky
Like the flames of wax candles,
And there comes, broken promise,
No moon or God's stars in mist.
A dark-bound boor it made me,
Unilluminating mist ;
No clear road under the sky,
A grey veil thwarts love's errand,
And thwarts me, keen my longing,
From reaching my slim-browed girl.

THE MIRROR

I'd not dreamed, burdensome bane,
My face not fine and handsome,
Till I lifted, lucid thing,
The glass : and see, it's ugly !

The mirror told me at last
That I am not good-looking.

The cheek for one like Enid
Turns sallow, it's scarcely flushed.
Glassy the cheek from groaning,
But a single, sallow bruise.
The long nose might be taken
For a razor : isn't it sad ?
Is it not vile, the glad eyes
Are pits completely blinded ?
And the worthless curly hair
Falls from the head in handfuls.

Heavy on me, evil fate :
It's either, in my judgment,
That I'm a swarthy quiver,
Foul sort, or the glass is bad.
If I, protracted passion,
Am at fault, may I be dead !
If the mirror's spotted face
Is at fault, then good riddance !

Pallid moon, round and mournful,
Full of magic, loadstone shape,
Faint colour, enchanted gem,
Constructed by magicians,
Dream of most fleeting manner,
Cold traitor and twin to ice,
Treacherous, harsh truth's servant,
May the mocking glass be burnt !

No one gave me a creased face,
If one should trust this mirror,
Except the girl of Gwynedd,
Famous for spoiling a face.

A GIFT OF WINE

Peter's Feast : I was eyeing,
In Rhosyr, where fine men flock,
What the well-off were wearing,
And Môn's crowds beside the sea.
And there, she is Gwynedd's sun,
In fine feather, an Enid,
Was a frail, pale, round-necked girl,
Splendid, refined, and comely ;
In that fairground my fine girl
Like Mary's living image,
And all, drawn by her beauty,
After her, colour of snow,
A marvel to the masses,
Heaven's gift, that sort of girl.
And I, struck sick and sleepless,
Stayed on watch to win the girl.
There's not been a gayer lad,
Guileless mind, small discretion.
Far from that flawless armful's
Neighbourhood, surely, I'd be,
Unless she came, grave woman,
To the bright stone balcony.

Twenty fellow-suitors turned
And came swarming about me.
To the lord who craves her's cost,
I tried the wine, fine steward,
Purchased, it gave no pleasure,
Two full gallons at one stroke.

'Leave, servant, this gay circle,
Take this to that lovely girl.
Race to her ear and whisper
To that queenly form, and swear
She's the maiden in Gwynedd
I love most, by God above.

'Make your way to her chamber ;
Say to her : "Greetings, fair maid !
Severe one, see, a present
For you, my beloved girl".'

'Is this not trash from the town ?
Boy, why do we not know you ?
It's foolish, unseemly thought,
If so, to ask who sent it.'

'Dafydd, lord of dear delight,
Dark grey man : I'm his envoy.
His fame has spread through Gwynedd ;
Hear him : he sounds like a bell.'

'On your feet, by the five wounds !
Where are you all ? And beat him !'

She took the town's sparkling wine,
On my lad's hair she splashed it !
That deed was my dishonour ;
Mary curse the bold fair dear !
If gravely she disgraced me
In that place, consort of rage,
Cloaked in her azure caddis,
May her foolish lip lack wine !
If I could, firmly coupled,
I'd leave her to Madog Hir.
She's not likely, bold vile guest,
To get an inn from Einon.

She, a seagull's fair colour,
Will see her ear with her eye
Before ever I will send
The girl scornful of passion,
Fair or foul, the gift of one
Spoonful of luke-warm water !

AN INVITATION TO DYDDGU

Maiden, refined and radiant,
Dyddgu of the smooth dark hair,
I, lair of secret longing,
Ask you to Manafan's dale.

No feeble bid befits you,
No glutton's bid to his hut,
No dish to reward reapers,
No meal mixing bright young grain,
No share of farmers' dinners,
No Shrove Tuesday fill of meat,
No Saxon spread for a friend,
No churl's son's first-shave feasting :
I promise naught, good ending,
But mead and a nightingale,
A soft-tuned brown nightingale
And a gay strong-voiced songthrush.

Frowning forest, green chamber
Of birches : what better house ?
While we're outdoors under leaves
Our strong birches will shield us ;
A loft for the birds at play,
Precious grove, so it's fashioned.
Nine trees of fine appearance
Compose the whole of the grove :
Below, a crooked circle,
A green belfry up above ;
Beneath them, delightful home,
Fresh clover, heaven's manna ;
Where two stay, crowds disturb them,
Or three, the space of an hour,
Where roebucks roam, reared on oats,
Where birds sing, it is splendid,
Where leaves are thick, blackbirds nest,

Where trees are fair, hawks fostered,
A fine new leafy dwelling,
Place for loving, heaven's here,
A green mansion, modest shade,
Cool, clear of smoke, near water,
A place unknown, tricky ground,
To any long-legged beggar.

There tonight, a wave's whiteness,
We two shall go, my fair girl.
We'll go — shall we ? — pale sweet face,
My girl, eyes like bright embers.

FOUR WOMEN

A girl gave her love to me,
The star of Nant-y-Seri,
Noble maid, not in false faith,
Graceful Morfudd, great-hearted.
Though I spent from wondrous zeal
My wealth, my compensation,
Though a pledge passed between us,
To her husband she was pledged.
But from rebuff, wondrous life,
God above, she's not sorry,
Then love for her, fear played false.
World's moon, I swore was ended.

When I loved the wife, weak vow,
Then, of the bald-head burgess,
The hunchback, show of servants,
A top man's wife, Robin Nordd's,
Ellen, eager for riches,
My treasure whose accent clings,
Queen of a, lady of wool,

House of cloth, gorse-fire country,
A loving man was needed,
I'm sad it could not be me.
She'd not accept, fair wave's face,
Song for nothing, strong honour.
With ease I had, all in hand,
Nothing simpler, good stockings ;
If I wish, white gossamer,
Motley, she makes it gladly.

I'm never, untroubled zest,
By God, without some payment,
Whether in words of high praise,
Or notion of sweet music,
Or gold if I give pleasure,
Or something, merry am I.
And then, though my lips may be
Weaving a song for Dyddgu,
Nothing, by God, 's my function,
But following fickleness.

A realm's queen, its sustenance,
The world knows, is the fourth one.
Not from my smooth prudent tongue,
Foam's hue, she or another
Hears her name or her birthplace,
Praise is due, or which she was.
No top man's lusty woman,
No man do I love as much
As the whitewashed fort's bright girl :
Goodnight to her, she's thankless.
The word is, loving's fruitless :
I'll win, I'll not spare, reward.
If she'd know one man's longing
For her sake, such would it be :
Were she bad, fair-cheeked beauty,
Enough to be hanged, fine prize,

More strongly, mine's a foe's pain,
Her praise I'll shape, Nyf's colour,
Fair her form, and all Gwynedd
Will praise her ; who has her's blest !

SUMMER

It grieves us, Adam's frail sons,
Flood of bliss, how brief's summer.
By the Lord, it is most foul,
How it ends, enter summer
And a smooth and spotless sky,
The glad sun's glow of summer,
An easy, sauntering breeze,
The whole world sweet in summer.

Splendid crop, unblemished flesh,
Out of old earth comes summer.
To grow, turning comely green,
Leaves on trees there is summer.
Seeing lovely hair, I'll laugh,
On a fair birch in summer.
Paradise, I'll shape its song,
Who'll not laugh when it's summer ?
I'll praise it persistently,
Sweet style, a prize is summer !

Beneath twigs, one fair as foam
I'll love, her daring's summer.
The cuckoo, at my request,
Will sing, new sun of summer,
Fine grey bird, I'll make her my
Vesper bell at mid-summer,
The fair clear-voiced nightingale
Fullfledged, bold, housed for summer,

The thrushcock, I'll flee from strife,
Sweetly babbling in summer.

Ovid's man, lovely long day,
Pays calls, bold speech, in summer.
Eiddig, Adam's unclaimed son,
Is unconcerned with summer :
Winter's made for one his age ;
The lovers' lot is summer.

And I beneath birches want
Only mantles of summer.
Round me I'll wear a fine web,
Bright cloak, fair hair of summer.
Ivy leaves will I untwine,
Long day's not cold in summer.
When I greet a gentle girl,
Glad our embrace in summer.

Song's of no use, sigh of cold,
Banned the sweet bard of summer.
Wind will not leave, I don clothes,
Trees fullfledged, ah for summer !
My heart, I make no excuse,
Yearns for fair skies in summer.
When come, in fall, winter here,
Frost and snow, ousting summer,
It grieves me, Christ, and I ask,
Too soon it's gone, 'Where's summer ?'

LOVE'S FEVER

A pretty girl's bewitched me,
Sweet Morfudd, godchild of May.
She'll get her proper greeting,
I'm fevered tonight with love.

She's sown in my breaking heart
Love's seed, a magic frenzy ;
The fruits of pain, here's my plaint,
Fair as day, she denies me.
Enchantress, lovely goddess,
Her speech puts a spell on me.
Careless when she is accused,
Careless of me, unfavoured.
Peace I'd have, luck and learning,
Today with my clever girl.
Innocent, unrecompensed,
I'm outlawed from her parish.
It's she who put, most painful,
Longing in her outlaw's heart :
Longer than sea on the strand
Lingers her outlaw's longing.
I've been fettered, my ribs nailed,
Affliction's been my fetter.

Unlikely, my chance of peace
With my shrewd gold-haired maiden :
Bad fevers were bred of this ;
Long life for me's unlikely.
She is Ynyr's own offspring ;
Lacking her I cannot live.

THE WIND

Welkin's wind, way unhindered,
Big blusterer passing by,
A harsh-voiced man of marvels,
World-bold, without foot or wing,
How strange that sent from heaven's
Pantry with never a foot,
Now you can race so swiftly
Over the hillside above.

F

You need no steed beneath you,
No bridge over stream, no boat ;
Forewarned, you remain undrowned,
A free and easy crossing.
Winnowing leaves, you steal nests,
None charge you, you're not halted
By armed band, lieutenant's hand,
Blue blade or flood or downpour.
No sheriff or troop takes you,
Pruner of the treetop plumes.
No mother's son slays, crime's tale,
Fire burns, deceit undoes you.

Unspied, in your wide bare bed,
Nest of storms, thousands hear you,
The sky's swift signatory,
Fine leaper of nine wild lands.
Godsent you skim over ground,
Roar of an oak-top broken,
A thirsty creature, sharp-set,
A great sky-trampling progress,
Huntsman in lofty snow-fields
Loudly heaping useless husks.
Tell me, incessant hymn-tune,
Your course, north-wind of the glen,
Tempest fettering the sea,
Lad romping on the seastrand,
Rhetorician, magician,
Sower, pursuer of leaves,
Hurling, laugher on hillsides,
Wild masts in white-breasted brine.

You fly the length of the world,
Hover tonight, hill's weather :
O wind, go to Uwch Aeron,
A bright beauty, a clear tune.

Do not stay, do not steer clear,
Do not fear Bwa Bach's poisoned
Complaints and accusations ;
Closed is that country to me.
Sad day for me when I set
My heart on golden Morfudd :
A girl has brought me exile ;
Run above her father's home.
Pound the door, make it unlock
Before day to my envoy.
If there is a way, find her
And moan the sound of my sigh.

You come from the zodiac ;
Tell my great-hearted darling
For as long as I may live
I am her faithful plaything.
Sad-faced am I without her
If truly she's not untrue.
Fly high, you'll see a beauty,
Fly low, find a road of sky.
Go to my pale blonde maiden,
Bounty of the sky, fare well.

A PRAYER TO SAINT DWYN

Saint Dwyn, tears fair as hoarfrost,
Well your golden image in
The candle-lit chancel knows
How to heal sorry wretches.
Who keeps vigil, holy time,
In your shrine, glowing Indeg,
No disease or dismal thought
May go with him from Llanddwyn.

Long the line of your suitors,
Anxious, in anguish, am I.
This breast with lover's longing
Is one rankling wound of love ;
Long pain of apprehension,
I know the signs, this is plague,
Unless I have, if I live,
Morfudd, look, my life's wasted.
Cure me, a far sweeter song,
Of feebleness and baseness.
Mingle this year love's message
With God's graces to a girl.
No need, undimmed gold image,
To fear sin, the snare of flesh.
God's deed He'll not, good His peace,
Undo : you'll not leave heaven.
No wench this year will see you
Whispering close at our sides.
Angry, hard-hearted Eiddig
Will not beat you, pure of heart.

Come, be silent, none suspect
Wrong of you, faithful virgin,
From Llanddwyn, sought by many,
To Cwm-y-glo, gem of Christ.
God's not denied you the gift
Of words : she'll not deny you.
Certain the work of prayers,
God calls you, dark your chaplet.
Let the Lord, your host, hinder,
Mindful, her husband's two hands,
Harsh the one who'd harass her,
When she trails me through May's leaves.
Saint Dwyn, if you'd arrange one
Tryst in May's woods, a long day,
Bard's gift, good, fair one, you'd be.
Saint Dwyn, you were not base-born :

Show by your gracious blessings,
You're no low wench, wise Saint Dwyn.

By the weighty grace you gained
Leading a life of penance,
By the rule, faith's devotion,
You established while you lived,
By the nun's life of splendour,
The pent body's purity,
By the soul, if it's needful,
Of brawny-armed Brychan Yrth,
Beseech, by your sanguine faith,
The Virgin's gem to save me.

THE BIRCH HAT

Birch hat, you'll be guarded well,
A source of grief for Eiddig,
Spoil of the trees, tryst's trophy,
Carved cover of forest twigs.
Bold am I, it's no marvel,
One who owns you knows your worth,
Woven of wood, it is flawless,
Mantle of May's leafy twigs.
With fine art you were plaited,
You're my store of courtesy.
God blesses you, easy praise,
Roof made of meadow birches,
Garland from a clear-voiced girl,
Circlet of bright green birch-leaves.

I'll wear, lean lad, though in flight,
This fine cowl of May's mantle.
Wisely and well I'll guard you,
Crown keeping out summer's glare,

Dell's fellows, bright green valley,
Fair birchwood in harmony,
Flawless golden girl's firm love,
May's miracles, rich bounty,
Shield from neglect and sorrow,
Cloak of an unclouded brow,
Prized growth, praiseworthy branches,
Collar of close-woven twigs.

Praise is due, fair roof of leaves,
Green round glad to be taken,
Love's artful hue, true token,
Wooded slope's cincture of hair,
No defects, finely fashioned,
The work of Morfudd Llwyd's hand.

A MOONLIT NIGHT

All the year long, hard problems
God sets to hinder a man.
No freehold have poor lovers
By night, by day, none at all.
After being hard provoked,
No nearer's grace, night bars it.
Vain the twigs of many groves,
I pine for a bright blossom.
Ovid's man will not venture,
I'm her dear, to her by day ;
Not much, I'm sure, my blessing,
My reward, while night stays bright.

In fair thick woods I've waited,
Sight blurred with fear, for a tryst.
Worse than the sun's the bright moon,
It is, it's large, so frigid ;

Broad and brilliant is the moon,
White fire, hard frosty weather.
Smooth flattery, should it stay,
Poor us, poor thief, who's spied on.
What's worse, the gift restricts him,
For a thief than a clear night?

It's torment, on each new twig
Blossoms of daylight brilliance.
It's the moon's rule each fortnight,
Night's its home beneath the sky,
To make its way from the dark,
Sober thought, on and on it
Goes, till both halves are perfect,
Sun, radiant night, of the stars.
It sways tides, lovely brightness,
A sun it is, to the ghosts.

From his bed, at ease, Eiddig,
By the moon, mind clear, above,
To my lair beneath fair twigs
Will see me at his border.
It helped the man, that florin,
Climbs between her and the sky.
Round it lay on my pathway,
Rowel of the cold wind's spur,
Frustrated lover's hindrance,
A slice from a loaf of ice.
Archthief of summer's thwarted,
Too bright to go to a girl.
Far on high it has its bed,
God's portion, in fair weather.

It perceives me, world's candle,
Hidden, it rises from cloud,
Semblance of a criss-cross sieve,
Lip acquainted with lightning,

Woman strolling the sky-road,
It's a thong, a cauldron's rim.
Broad as the earth its borders,
Like a camp for wild and tame.
Meadows of stars it measures,
Compass of the pale bright sky.

Sunless day, a false coin came
To drive me from my refuge.
Glowing face, before bright dawn
Glad I'd be if it darkened.
That I may send love's envoys,
No vain words, to my dear's home,
While night stays, snug and splendid,
God darken the world outside.
A fair law, for our master,
By the Lord, the light of day,
And night for us, our portion,
For the two of us, the dark.

THE THREE PORTERS

Three porters, angry noises,
A nuisance, Eiddig's three aids,
Were trained to fear me greatly :
A sad encounter I had.

The first in that hateful place
Of the three, Eiddig's porter,
Was a loud, persistent hound :
I was rebuked, fierce barking.
And second the angry door,
Grief's comrade, with its creaking.
Third, mine is constant penance,
Barring me from my reward,

Was a sickly, cranky hag,
Her day will come, his servant.
Were the night, dream of heaven,
As long as ten, restless hag,
She'd sleep, her bed's flea-ridden,
Not an hour, unsound her bones.
Soon there's a feeble wailing
Of hip, misshapen, and hand,
And aches in her two elbows,
Her bruised shoulder, and her knee.

Last night, sad black night, I went,
A clumsy man, to Eiddig's,
Of high talent, intending
To visit a gem, a fair moon.
Bard's jail, as I was going
Carelessly towards the dark door,
There leapt, he longed to mark me,
From the pigsty a red dog.
He growled his surly greeting,
He chewed at my horse-hair cloak,
He ripped, fierce fort, the man's dog,
Weak the stitch, my whole mantle.
I pushed, a pan's racket,
The oak door, it went berserk.
It clamoured like geese cackling ;
If I dared close it, woe's me !
Blushing bard, I heard the hag,
Worst of luck, in her corner,
Insisting (isn't it baffling ?)
To the master up above :
'The heavy door stands open,
The dog is making a din.'

In vile mood I fled back to
The door, foul dog at my heels.

I ran, I did not stand there,
By the wall, I felt a chill,
Around the gleaming fortress,
Searching for my shining gem.
I shot love's shafts, pain's burden,
Through the wall to the slim girl.
And she in turn shot to me
From her bright breast love's greeting.
Gladdened, love did not fail me,
By the wall with the slim girl,
I grieved, I spoke my anger,
In need, against Eiddig's door.

Though he can, lost conjunction,
With high hedge and hag and hound
Exclude me, he clings closely,
From his, Eiddig's, house and home,
God has granted me freely
The fields and the full-branched woods.

A WISH FOR EIDDIG

There left today superbly
The guard of generous Rhys,
Sworn brothers, foster brothers
And cousins, my yearning's keen,
Of mine, to trade blows with France —
From the South, Mary, speed them —
Proud hawks of the battle's breach,
Leaders of combat's brothers.

Son of scorn, there's a hornet
Along, if you let him, men,
Abominable foe to
The girl's bard, and the world's bards.

One eye, tyrant's oppression,
And one ear's on this fair limb,
Dull-witted horn of deceit,
Bane of the girl, her bailiff.
From a vile death many times
I have fled, you remember,
From his closed cage of elders
And his men, that reaping-crew.
For him, and for his household,
A fistful of devil's shit !

If he boards, piggy creature,
The wild ship in raging waves,
She will not stay still for long,
Her sail brimful of briny,
Streaming white wall her headdress,
The swift channel's Gascon mare.
She'll not venture, not voyage,
The scoundrel, the wretch on board.
Let him be shoved, beaver's rump,
Overboard near the seacoast.

Generous wave, wing of brine,
To you I'd be indebted,
Strand's child, sea-chamber's marvel,
Never leave that vile old man.
Shaft of ocean, tide's stabber,
Nine hungry waves suck him in.

Wave to wave, bird of quicksand,
Should the black babbler reach France,
Many meshes that are there,
May a snare be his finish.
Concentrate, sturdy business,
On killing him, do me good,
Do not let the hollow ship
Part me from South Wales' jewel.

And you, crossbowman, hurry,
Hurler of good solid wood,
Loose the short wooden stirrup
And shoot : so what if he's vexed ?
Wound the thief in the temple,
Shatter his dream, make it swift.
Thrust through him, do not misfire,
Send a second bolt through him.
Look for, shooter of straight shafts,
His lank and scrawny whiskers.
Shabby beard, a fennel bush,
Time's come, good were his taking.
Sweet for us if he stays there,
Twelve calamities to him !
Unbind a bard, this is fine,
Let him never come back home.

Venomous, jealous muzzle,
Vile face, should he seek to come,
Let a foe's zeal, loud outcry,
The black robber, send him home.

AUBADE

Loudly have I been moaning,
The night before last was long.
That night was, bright lovely girl,
Eight nights in one, my darling ;
And short the night, says the judge,
She grants with no denial.

Last night, discreetly, I stayed,
Fair Nyf, with heaven's candle,
Recompensed for loss of sleep,
Busy beside my sweetheart.

When I held her most tightly,
At my full stretch, dark her brows,
Highest veil, restless ardour,
Ah, dear God ! look, the day dawns.

'Rise,' said she, gleaming curtain,
'Conceal this : there's the fair sign.
Despair of all your kinsmen,
Go to the devil : day breaks.'

'Fair darling, slim and flawless,
That is false, this is the truth :
The moon of God's own giving
And the circle of stars is this.
This, if I name it rightly,
Is only a fancied day.'

'Familiar words, if that's true,
Then why is the crow cawing ?'
'It's the ticks tormenting her
Keep her awake — she kills them.'

'There are dogs howling in town
And quarrelling with others.'

'Trust me when I deny it,
It's the noise dogs make at night.'

'Stop with your bard's pretences ;
Pain's the tale when prudence fails :
On your way, you destroyer,
Venture into day, it's prime.
For Christ's sake, rise in quiet,
And open that heavy door.
Too heavy fall the footsteps,
Bold the hounds : run to the wood.'

'Ah God ! the grove's not distant,
And I can outrun a hound.
Unspied I'll stay uncaptured,
God willing, upon these grounds.'

'Tell me, good faithful poet,
For God's sake, if you'll return.'

'When night comes, darling, surely,
I'm your nightingale, I'll come.'

THE STAR

A foam-white girl disturbs me,
God knows the mind of each man.
Should my love for her move me,
My bright dear, to visit her,
I've small mind to commission
A proud herald to her home,
Nor to bribe a sluttish hag,
Grey and bold, for love's message,
Nor bear lanterns before me,
Or wax torches, when it's late.
No, I'll sleep home in daylight
And walk abroad when it's night.
None will see, none will know me,
I'm reckless, for us it's day.
I have, there's no denying,
Lest I lose my way tonight,
Candles of the world's own Lord
To guide me to my jewel.

Blessed be the Maker's name
By whose craft stars were fashioned,
For there is nothing brighter
Than the small, round, pure-white star.

The high heaven's light it is,
A clear and steady candle.
This candle will not grow dim,
And no deceit can steal it ;
Fall winds will not blow it out,
Heaven's roof's holy wafer ;
Flood waters will not drown it,
Woman on watch, dish of saints.
No robber's hands will reach it,
Base of the Trinity's bowl ;
It's not proper for a man
To seek a pearl of Mary's.
It will light every region,
Coin of minted yellow gold.
It is the light's true buckler,
The shape of the sky's bright sun.

It will show me unhidden,
Fine gold gem, where Morfudd is.
Christ on high will put it out,
And send it, but not shortly,
Its shape like a round white loaf,
To sleep in the sky's shadow.

MAY AND JANUARY

Welcome, sweet greenwood chorus,
Summer's May, my longed-for month,
Mighty knight rewarding love,
Green-mailed lord of wild forests,
Comrade of courtship and birds,
Mind turned on lovers' yearning,
Herald of a hundred trysts,
Loving courtly encounters.

And great, by Mary, will be
That flawless month, May, 's coming,
Intent, hot for his honour,
On conquering each green glen.
Close cover, cloak of highways,
Clothes each place in its green web.
When the war with frost is past,
Meads flourish, thick-leaved mantles,
Green will be, my credo chirps,
May's paths, no longer April's,
Then will come to the oak-tops
The cheeping of baby birds,
Cuckoos in every quarter,
And songsters, and long fine days,
And white mist, the wind dying,
Shielding the heart of the glen ;
Then come bright skies, fine evenings,
Lovely trees, green gossamer,
And many birds in the woods,
And fresh leaves on the branches,
And thoughts of my gold Morfudd,
And the three-score turns of love.

Most unlike the dark harsh month
Punishing all for loving,
Causing dismal rain, short days,
And wind plundering woodlands,
And feebleness, mortal fear,
And trailing cloaks, and hailstones,
And roiling of tides, and cold,
And in the brooks brown torrents,
And swollen-sounding rivers,
And rousing of day to wrath,
And the sky sullen, frigid,
Its colour cloaking the moon.
May he, wishing is easy,
Be doubly cursed for a lout.

THE SKYLARK

Strong prayers are the skylark's
Who spirals aloft each day,
Dawn riser, rich spate of song,
Sky's portion, April's porter.

Cheerful voice, steersman of songs,
Yours are sweet lanes, fair labours,
Song shaped above hazel groves,
Brown wings' modest achievement.
Yours the spirit, pleasant task,
And high-flown words for preaching,
Strong song from the fount of faith,
Privileged in God's presence.
High you soar, Kai's own power,
And on high you sing each song,
Bright spell near the wall of stars,
A far high turning journey.
Be sparing, you have mounted
High enough : the prize is yours.

Let each good creature praise his
Creator, pure radiant lord.
Praising God as He bade you,
Thousands listen, do not cease.
Lyrist of love, where are you ?
Lucid voice in garb of grey.
Your song is sweet and merry,
Melodious russet muse.
Chanter of heaven's chapel,
Fair is faith, great is your skill.
All honour, harmonious song,
Broad is your cap, brown-tufted.

Set your course for well-known skies,
Singer, the wild white country.

G

One above gives you a sure
Light when the day is longest.
When you arise to worship,
The triune God grants you this :
Not a treetop sustains you
Above the world, sweet your speech,
But the true Father's blessings,
Miraculous providence.

Teacher of praise dawn to dark,
Descend, may God protect you.
My fair brown bird, if you'll bear,
My fellow bard, love's message,
Bring greetings to a beauty,
Gifted with light, Gwynedd's moon.
And beg one of her kisses
To bring to me here, or two.
Lord of the sky's chartless sea,
Hover by her hall yonder.
Would I were with her always,
Eiddig's rage, my break of day.

Such value is on your head
He will not dare to kill you.
Should he try it, fierce temper,
Eiddig's bane, you'll stay alive.
Wide from your perch you'll circle,
Far beyond his hand and bow.
Cross-country tramp, sad bowman,
His great aim will go awry ;
Wicked his wrath, above him
Wheel as his arrow goes by.

THE JUDGMENT

I am Morfudd's own poet,
Costly task, I shaped her song.
By the Man who rules today
My head aches for my fair one,
And care pierces my forehead ;
I die for a golden girl.

When death comes, the bones' summons,
With his whizzing crossbow bolts,
Immense the devastation,
And an end to human speech.
The Three, forestalling lament,
Great the tumult, and Mary
My crooked course may pardon,
Amen, and I'll sing no more.

THE SWORD

Lengthy you are, grey figure,
By God, sword, along my leg.
Your blade allows, fine bold lord,
No disgrace to your comrade.
I keep you at my right hand ;
May the Lord keep your keeper.
My plaything, how you glitter,
I'm the master, you're my might.

My dear's husband hates my life,
Fierce his attack, sly schemer.
Tight-lipped, ill-famed, ignoble,
Vicious, mad scowl, like an ox,
Sometimes he's mute, good temper,
And sometimes he threatens me.

While you're mine, fierce lord of force,
For his threat, mighty weapon,
A curse upon his mattress,
Burned be your lord if he flees,
On horseback, shameful notion,
Or on foot for fear of him,
Till scorn's two fierce words bring me
Your moment, Eiddig's bane.

Stab till the enemy runs,
Cyrseus, my two-edged shearer.
You're the hand's finest handle ;
No rust on you, you are flint.
Boon of battle-bedlam's crows,
Flee, Deira : two firm edges.
Lightning flash near a meadow,
I'll keep you housed in your sheath.
You're keenly fit for my foe,
Fine sword, sharp-grooved and shining.

Firm keen blade, here's my credo,
Where I give you a free hand :
Lest there be in the grove's keep
A night-time kite to catch us,
A twirling taper's splendour,
Whirl, steel, like a wheel of fire.
Hide not, shield of Cuhelyn,
From my hand if the man comes.
Bold circle, bright assertion,
You're a battle, comely steel.
From wicked men this guards me,
Needful sword, curved Hawt-y-Clyr.

A long way I'll be outlawed
In the woods, I and my girl.
My outlaw's life's not boorish,
Should she ask, not for true love.

My pedigree contents me ;
Thick my tracks near my dear's home.
No fugitive, I'm Ovid,
Courtly is a loving heart.

THE RIVAL

Slim girl, bear my displeasure,
Since summer, grieve at the gift.
Hard smithcraft, my grief also,
Fair sweetheart, making it yours.
Grieved the girl, whom rage follows,
Rebuked by the jealous man.
Grieved the one, pain of hot wax,
Tears' floods, jealousy torments.

I've shaped song to your beauty,
Costly the task, care is mine.
Greater my pain, man's revenge,
Than his pain who is chained to
A stone perch, no wall's snugness,
For plotting to stab the Pope,
Lest of you, firm denial,
A true tale's told, glowing girl.

There is, too much grief, say some,
A proud lad, young and handsome,
I'm a sharer, you fancy
For a tryst, to lie with you.
Though he's dashing, clear conscience,
A well-bred peacock worth praise,
Before he's yours, distant risk,
Bear in mind, twin to Indeg,
He'll not suffer, I'm wrathful,
From wind and rain, dainty face,

What I've suffered to seek you,
How often on bold journeys
I've travelled to where you were.
He'll not go straying, sweetheart,
At night for you, starry-hued,
Across twined chains of brambles,
Guileless girl, as I have gone.
Nor stay beneath, slight torrent,
A merry girl's weeping roof
With mind and mouth for wooing,
Sad he'll leave, as I have stayed.
He will not show on his cheeks
Warm water from true sorrow
This year in such a torrent,
Passion's Eigr, as I have shown.
He'll not sing within lords' woods
Praises for you till doomsday
A hundredth part, ford's foaming,
Of the canon I have sung.

Firm you are, denying trysts ;
Innocent are your answers.
If you're the one proves guilty
Of too sly an other man,
Christendom's bards will declare
Of you, pebbled ford's colour :
'A curse on you, merry girl,
If you, hue of stream spuming,
My fair, comely, courteous dear,
Treat badly, radiant maiden,
Your bard, seething shallows' hue,
Your own love who's possessed you.'

A SIMILE FOR MORFUDD

I wait for a soft-voiced girl,
Snowdrift glow by a meadow.
God knows the girl is lustrous,
Brighter than a crest of foam,
Hue of a bright, booming wave,
Sun's brightness, she is lovely.
She knows what my love-song's worth,
Sun's splendour in the heavens.
Queen of all, fine fur mantle,
She can mock a wretched man.
Sweet Morfudd, sad the foolish
Bard who loves her, hard to tame.
Web of gold, this girl, sad he
Whose loud lament's well-fashioned.

How sly she is and cunning,
More than any : she's my love.
One time my splendid darling
Shows herself at church and court ;
Another, fine lime-white fort,
Bright Morfudd stays in hiding,
Like the beneficent sun,
The nurse of warmth's dominion.
Praised be her splendid purpose,
Bright spendthrift merchant of May.
Long the wait for bright Morfudd,
Mary's mirror, clear and fair.

To the broad earth's low border
Comes the sun like a blithe girl,
Comely creature of the day,
Shepherdess of the heavens.
Then later, close conflicting,
Come thick clouds about her head,

Warring, how much it hurts us,
On the sun to dim her face,
Till there's small need of darkness,
Like bitter pain, when it's night.
Brimming the dark grey heavens,
Mournful picture, planet's home :
Hard for any to know there,
That ball of God, where she goes.
There's not a hand can touch her,
Nor take a grip on her brow.
Next day once more she rises,
From the world's roof sending light.

No different, wrath's ration,
Is Morfudd's hiding from me :
Once she's come down from the sky,
Making assault in daylight,
She hides, her frown is lovely,
Behind her cold husband's door.

I sought passion in the plain
Of Y Penrhyn, love's dwelling.
There is where one sees daily
A bright girl : each night she flees.
Hand's no nearer to touching
In the hall, it's been my death,
Than are, girl sung so dearly,
Men's hands to holding the sun.
There's no better, brighter face,
The sun blazing upon her.
If one this year's the fairest,
Fairest, lord's child, is our sun.

Why, here's a wish that's twisted,
Cannot this one rule the night,
The other's splendid sunshine,

Fine light, give lustre to day ?
Should both these faces be shown
Circling the world's four corners,
It would be a strange legend
If night came while this girl lived.

MORFUDD'S FICKLENESS

Cruel I'd call your changing,
Fair tidbit, before tonight.
I've a mind, moment of strength,
Versed in sleight, to revile you.
Madawg Lawgam's child Morfudd,
By the Pope, I know the cause
You left me in this manner,
Sadly alone on the strand.

While I could, I've not wronged praise,
Play the part of your husband,
Transgression of right, love's spell,
My scourge, did you not love me ?
And now I've been found wanting,
Deep wound, I've no place to turn.
Well-shaken, power of pain,
Your mind by the Black Idler.
You've replaced me, it's a blow,
Glowing white star's complexion,
Like the man, specious status,
Who's keeping under the yoke
Two pair of perfect oxen
For a single strong sure plough :
Should he plough my coarse-grained cheek,
Wild headland, he'll keep changing,
Today the one, God's fair day,
Next day the other, needless.

As a ball, rebuke's harsh word,
Is played with, my sworn lover,
Praise your due, your form's pursued
From hand to hand, bright image.
Lasting gifts, dear lovely face,
Such is your mind, Dyfr's colour.

A squire in two fine garments,
And both of them tight as bark,
Once swam with perseverance
Unrewarded, hard bargain.
Who may do good in birchwoods,
If she choose, let him come in ;
Who's done it, proven brother,
Out of her hands let him go.

Let him repent who loves you,
You cast me off, sated soon.
It's true, a cask's shoved aside,
Cast empty to a corner.

MORFUDD AND DYDDGU

Grief is mine, woeful figure,
Ceaseless, that I knew not love
Before her time to marry
For a splendid, slender maid,
Peerless her gifts, proper, wise,
Refined and sweet and clever,
As eloquent as an heir,
Untamed, dainty and truthful,
A rounded form, without fuss,
Talent trained to perfection,
Lovely, bright lively Indeg,
Virgin land, an ox am I,

Lover who never wavers,
Golden wand, glowing her brow,
Such is, long celebration,
Dyddgu of the smooth dark brow.

Most unlike that is Morfudd,
But like this, a glowing coal :
Loving some who censure her,
Stubborn girl, she'll be sorry,
Possessing, proper honour,
House and husband, lovely girl.
My flight is no less frequent
At midnight for that girl's sake
From one near her blue-glassed home
Than by day, I'm an athlete ;
The stern man, the senseless speech,
Beating his hands together,
His shout loosed daily, swift lust,
Stolen's his children's mother.

Feeble man, devil take him
For shouting ! Why does he wail,
Ah, poor him, simpleton's howl,
Up to God, that she's spellbound.
A young beast's far-heard bawling,
A foolish task's his false text.
He played the freak and coward,
Wailing of the slender girl.
All of South Wales he wakens
By calling, a sweetheart's kite.
Unskilful, no lack of discord,
Not pretty to hear, not sweet,
A man screeching, raucous horn,
Like a crow for his comrade.

Wicked's this one wakeful cry,
Liar, about what's borrowed.

If I bought, bright loyal heart,
Me a wife, foolish measure,
Sad prickster, for an hour's peace,
By rights, I'd let him have her,
So poorly, widow's portion,
Sour man, can he play the game.

In one word, I choose Dyddgu
To love — if she's to be had.

LOVE IN SECRET

I've learned to steal love swiftly,
Courtly, clandestine, and bold,
The best way in seemly words
To speak of love that's secret.
Such secret sharer's weakness,
Finest theft of a man's love,
While we're in the midst of crowds,
The girl and I, two idlers,
With no one, a pleasant talk,
Suspecting what we're saying.

For a long while, in times past,
Trustful, we took our pleasure.
Now, by ways more restricted,
We share, fearing scorn, three words.
One wicked tongue has ruined
By its looseness, worst of luck,
Hurling its words of slander
At us, blameless names, us both.
Fine once, if there was warning,
While in hiding we conspired.

I walked there, I worshipped leaves,
Her home, while green leaves lasted.

Delightful, dear, was the time,
Our life led in one birch-grove,
Locked together, no short while,
Woodland cell, snug together,
Strolled on the strand together,
Lingered together near woods,
Planted birches together,
Together wove fair trees' plumes,
Talked about love together,
Gazed together at lone glades.
Uncensured task for my girl,
To walk the woods together,
Stay straight-faced, smile together,
Laugh together lip to lip,
Fall together near the grove,
Shun crowds, complain together,
Share life, together drink mead,
Share love, lying together,
Sustain true love together
In secret — I'll say no more.

BEAUTY'S RUIN

The girl I'd call my gold dear,
My lovely, lucent darling,
I've a mind, fearful prudence,
By God's grace spurning deceit,
To have done, my sweet greets me,
With her, birches beckon her.
What use is my pursuing?
Let this be the hour it ends.

Ruined has been, strict censure,
Her hue for many a day.
I'm helpless, the skill's not there,
Nothing can cure her colour.

I believe, mine is torment,
That I know, mine is more care,
The thing it is that happened
To afflict her pretty cheeks.
Smooth Enid, it was Eiddig's
Breath of wrath from his black mouth,
When he loosed, a ruthless man's
Base act, she had Eigr's beauty,
His breath like a peat-bog's smoke
Round her (why won't she scrub it ?).
Grief's like a gripping fetter
Leaving that churl with the girl.

A varnished image of wood,
A noble's English carving,
Sordid safeguard, twisted thief,
A sputtering lamp soils it.
An English fur, fine enough,
In peat smoke will grow filthy.
A mist in the air will steal
All the sun's comely colour.
A broad-branched oak, wooden groyne,
At the sea's edge will wither.

I went to, strong compulsion,
The girl's home while she was fair.
Love's restrictive stewardship,
Though fair, not a father's house.
He knows how to make her face
Hateful, she was my sweetheart.
It's best for wretched Eiddig,
Black cur, if the girl's not fair.
The grime from his mouth has marred
My comely sweeting's colour.
By the Lord, grace was needed
For safeguard : she was too fair.

THE MAGPIE

Sick I was, for a girl's sake,
In a grove chanting love-charms,
One day, fervent burst of song,
Mild skies, early in April,
On green twigs the nightingale,
In gaps of leaves the blackbird,
Woodland bard in wooded rooms,
The thrush on the green treetop
Before rain loudly singing
Gold notes from a green-leaved screen,
And the skylark, tranquil voice,
Brown-hooded smooth-voiced songbird,
Straining his strength in soaring
With a song to heaven's heights,
From the bare plain, gentle prince,
He climbs in mounting spirals,
And I, a slim girl's poet,
Jubilant in a green grove,
The worn heart reminiscing,
And the soul renewed in me
With the joy of seeing trees,
Lusty life, in new garments,
And shoots of grain and grapevine
After shining rain and dew,
And green leaves above the glen,
And white tips on the thorntree :
By heaven, there was also
The magpie, world's shrewdest bird,
Building, beauty's betrayal,
In the tangled heart of the hedge,
With leaves and clay, a proud nest,
Her mate as her assistant.

Said the magpie, harsh complaint,
Haughty beak on the thornbush :

'Such fuss, sour foolish singing,
Old man, you make by yourself.
You're better off, by Mary,
Near a fire, greyhaired old man,
Than here amidst dew and rain,
In the green grove's cold showers.'

'Stop your noise, leave me in peace
Until the time for trysting.
Great love for a faithful girl
Causes me this commotion.'

'It's no use, your serving lust,
Poor feeble greyhaired halfwit.
Foolish sign of love's function,
Raving about a bright girl.'

'And you, magpie, black your beak,
Infernal bird, fierce-tempered,
You have, wasted your visit,
More toil and a tedious task,
Your nest like a heap of gorse,
Crammed, creel of withered branches.
You've pied feathers, how pleasant,
Painful looks, and a crow's head,
Motley you are, fine colour,
An ugly court, a hoarse voice.
Every outlandish language
You've learned, black and speckled wing.
Then, magpie, black is your head,
Help me, if you speak wisely.
Give me the finest counsel
You have for my feebleness.'

'I could give you good counsel,
Before May : act, if you will.
You've no right, bard, to a girl ;

For you there's but one counsel :
Solemn verse, be a hermit,
Foolish man, and love no more.'

Now I swear, God's my witness,
When I see the magpie's nest,
Because of this I'll leave her
Not an egg, no, nor a chick.

MORFUDD GROWN OLD

God grant the long-maned friar,
Drooping crow, long life and grace.
No peace for those who'd blaspheme
The friar's shadow figure,
The lord whom Rome should honour,
Bare feet, hair a nest of thorns.
The world-strolling robe's a snare,
A crossbar, the soul's blessing.

Mass-priest, eloquent chanter,
Kite, well he sings, of great God.
Privileged his charterhouse,
A ram of heaven's ruler,
Smooth speech flowing from his mouth,
Lively lip, Mary's magus.
He spoke of, tough-minded talk,
Her hue who's false but seldom :

'Put on, queen of a hundred,
A cambric and crystal blouse.
Wear, not undressed for a week,
A long gown, smooth and dainty.
"Well-born I was, a Deirdre ;
Blacker the clothes, double grief."'

H

Grey baldpate, smooth-tongued friar,
Of her beauty, thus he spoke.
As a young fool, were I Pope,
I'd not break off with Morfudd.
And now, grief's accusations,
The Maker's disfigured her
Till there's not one flourishing
Lock of hair, grey and faded,
Playing false, plaguing beauty ;
Her hue's less lasting than gold.
Queen of the land of no sleep,
Men's beautiful betrayal,
Splendid she was, sleepless life,
A dream she is : life's fleeting.
Besom on a brewer's floor,
Pale elder almost barren.

Tonight I'll not, so stricken,
Sleep a wink unless I'm there.
Blow of love for a maiden,
Old thief like a cry in sleep.
Enchantingly was she formed,
A pale enchanting bandit.
Old arm of a Gael's mangnel,
Cold summerhouse, she was fair.

THE RUIN

'Broken hut, with gaping holes,
Between moorland and meadow,
Sad are those, so they thought you,
Who once saw a festive home,
And see today, battered house,
A broken roof and rafters ;
And once by your lovely wall
A day passed, care was banished,

Within you, more delightful
Than you are now, scabby roof,
When I saw, I bore bright praise,
One so fair in your corner,
A girl, a noble darling,
Fair flower who lay with me,
Each arm, sweet the girl's embrace,
Entwined about the other,
The girl's arm, fine-grained snowflakes,
Beneath her dear poet's ear,
And my arm, simple tactics,
Under the comely girl's ear.
To your new wood sweet pleasure,
But today is not that day.'

'I moan, shelter's magic speech,
The wild wind in its passage.
Bred in the east a tempest
Battered at the wall of stone.
The sighing, an angry tide,
Of the south wind unroofed me.'

'Did the late wind play havoc?
Well it thrashed your roof last night;
It ripped your lathing awry:
Life's a fearful illusion.
Your corner, mine's that ingle,
My couch once, is no bed now.
You stood proudly yesterday
Snug above my dear sweetheart;
By Peter, you have today,
Plain tale, no door, no pillar.
Foolish riddle, often asked,
Is this torn hut mere fancy?'

'The household's long gone under
The cross, Dafydd.   They did well.'

THE END OF LOVE

A fickle heart has languished,
Love worked treason in my breast.

Once I was, my hundred wounds,
In my youth, I was lusty,
No feebleness, no torment,
A vassal at love's command,
Servant of song, sound of limb,
Ripe for trysts, bold and brilliant,
Bard of idle bubbling songs,
Most gay, loaded with language,
In splendid shape, free of flaws,
Merry and brisk and handsome.

Now at last, swift is distress,
I wither, weak with sorrow.
Wasted the arrogant ways,
Wasted the flesh, grief shakes me.
Wasted away is the voice,
And my prowess, hard downfall.
Wasted the muse of fair girls,
Wasted talk of love's trouble.

Rises in me, song in mind,
No glad purpose or passion,
No merry talk about them,
No love — but should a girl ask. . . .

Gruffudd ab Adda

THE MAYPOLE

Green birch, your hair has withered,
Long an outlaw from the slope.
Fine lance fostered in woodlands,
Green veil, you've betrayed your grove.

Inn for me and love's envoy
Was your close, in May's short nights.
Many once, hateful journey,
The tunes from your fine green twigs,
Songs of all sorts, well-fashioned,
I heard in your bright green home ;
Herbs of all kinds grew under
Your leaves amid hazel shoots,
When to a maiden's pleasure
You dwelt last year in the grove.

You think of love no longer,
Deaf stay your branches above.
For folly's sake forsaking
The green field, despite the cost,
From hill and height of honour
To town in a swift exchange.
Though your resting place be good,
Idloes town, crowded concourse,
Not good, my birchtree, to me
Your theft, your throngs, your dwelling ;
Not good for you there, green-cheeked,
Your place, for bearing green leaves.

Green-plumed each city garden,
Was it not, birch, rudely done,
To bring you here to wither,

107

Sad pole near the pillory ?
In leaftime, had you not come
To stand in the dry crossroad,
Though you're pleasing there, they say,
Better, tree, the brook's heaven.
Not a bird will sleep or sing,
Shrill chirp, on your fair branches,
So constant, dark wood's daughter,
The crowd's noise about your tent.
Savage wound, no more grass grows
Where the town tramps beneath you
Than once on the windswept way
Of the first man and woman.

You've been made to deal in trade,
You're like a market-woman :
Fairgoers, merry glitter,
Point their fingers at your pain,
Old fur and one pale garment,
Amidst petty merchandise.
No more, near your sister's side,
Ferns conceal your bold seedlings ;
No privacy, no secrets,
No shelter, beneath your eaves ;
Nor will you shield, piercing glance,
The primroses of April,
Nor will thought come of fetching
A fine bard, for the glen's birds.

God, we grieve, lean cold country,
Sudden fear, for you're ensnared.
Taller than noble Tegwedd
You tower, fine is your crest.
Make your choice, captive branches,
Foolish is your city life,
To leave for your home hillside,
Or to wither there in town.

THE THIEF OF LOVE

I've gone eight times, painful cry,
To that wood, wasted journeys,
Out there like one who's witless
Keeping house without a fire.
Easy for me, fine prowess,
By God, before the day dawns,
To steal for her sake swiftly
To the far side of the wood.
Woodland dawn discontents me,
A man who's walked far for love ;
I despair, it destroys me,
Woodland sun that once poured wine.

If as I run some spy me
Near her place where pain's my pay,
There am I, battle-netted,
An arch-thief, says greybeard's son.
I'm no thief in a hayloft
Shunning the dazzle of day :
I'm a thief, bound by a wound,
Not of steed but of sweetheart ;
No thief of a ram this night,
Thief of a maid, sweet moment ;
No thief of a cattle pen,
Thief of her beneath branches ;
Thief of a bold enchantress,
Thief of painful miles, not mills,
Thief in pain of one not mine,
Thief of pure love, not purses.
I'm thief of not one hoofed beast,
I'm not a man long sought for :
The theft of love enthralls me,
Thief of, pain-fettered, a girl.

Madog Benfras

THE SALTMAN

I bore, costly compulsion,
A load of salt for my sun,
Trading places, reckless task,
With the kind-hearted saltman.

The fierce bold buck I spoke of,
Of Eiddig's long memory,
Complained to God, concerning
The dark watchman posted there,
Frantic, lest I be spotted
Having words with that fair hand.
The frail old fellow had my
Fine saddle and gentle steed ;
Clever notion, my portion,
Sore burden for my thin back,
The basket, complete with salt,
Covered with hide, to carry,
And a cudgel made of fir,
A strap of shiny leather,
A pouch that held mouldy meal,
An old cap, cups to measure,
And a soft green-grass cushion
Between my back and the pack.

I took a path, close lookouts,
That led up to Eiddig's house.
I went, it was a wonder,
From dunghill to great dark house,
Stood with the nasty basket
Under my arms, filthy load,
Shouting 'Salt !', shoulders coated,
Clear praise of salt-water salt.

Then rose a volley of oaths
From the ill-mannered villeins,
Mocking me with metaphors,
And hounds howled in the kennel.

What with churls' music and hounds,
And me amidst the tumult,
The fair goddess awakened,
Free with wine, white as a wave :
'Faithful Mary ! speak, maiden,
Good you are, and dear to me,
Quite plainly, shepherds' brawling,
What is this noise in the hall ?'

'There came, into senseless snares,
One who was like a saltman,
And the household, barren brawl,
Resounding music, mocked him,
And he, steady rebuttal,
Will not let one insult pass.'

'What's he like, cause of clamour,
Why this row with foolish churls ?'

'An adulterer disguised,
That is the sort, I think so.
Never, I know man's longing,
Was there saltman in such shape,
Nor clothes to thwart exposure,
Spies at work, like those on him.'

'Without one person knowing,
Gentle maid, the course I take,
Ask this man with his basket
To enter my chamber here.'

'He'll come,' said she, love-minded,
'God knows he will come for me.'

I entered with the basket
On my back, foolish my thoughts,
Into, passion was patient,
Her bedroom, beautiful girl.
I went to the girl's bedside,
I greeted the sweet one well.

'Put down your deceitful pack,
Most crafty love, good welcome.'

From the fair of skin, kindness
Was mine, and not selling salt :
A kiss, my girl bright as day,
Contention with each other.
Long life to the sweet-voiced gem,
Love's name, graceful beguiler.

Llywelyn Goch ap Meurig Hen

THE SKULL

THE BARD   Perfect skull, whom none will praise,
Pock-marked, withered-up headpiece,
Secret shame, foe of the fair
Wanton whose pale skin withered,
No gold does your cheeks homage,
Grave of sorry, mortal flesh.
Who placed you, impolitely,
Setting you to mock at me,
Out of vile, spiteful hatred,
On the wall there, dreary wretch?

THE SKULL   There's no nose, only ruins,
There is neither lip nor tooth,
There's no ear left, foul fracas,
There's no brow nor brilliant glance,
There's not an eye is left me,
And not a breath in my mouth.
Naught remains of eyes but dust
And pits brimful of blackness,
No hair, there is no mantle,
No skin to cover my face.

THE BARD   Much mortified is our land,
Cold sight, to look upon you.
Make, to conceal your forehead,
Your way to your bed of clay.
Allow, chilling all the rest,
Me my clever cywyddau.

THE SKULL   I have, I will not go back,
Lain long in a field's belly,
In fear, hiding my favour,
With the worms crowding me close.

113

I'll keep, though I may not drink,
My place, warning my parish.
From my niche I preach better
Than Saint Austin, or as well ;
There's no man skilled at hoodwinks
May look upon me and laugh ;
Grief of man, who will ask me,
Face of pain, to give him birth ?
Clean contrary to feasting,
The sight of my naked skull,
Where once could be seen like silk
Auburn hair in small ringlets,
A glowing, soft, smooth forehead,
A falcon's eye and fair brows,
Lips skilled in conversation,
A fair, sweet, neatly shaped nose,
Pretty gums' honeyed language,
Clever courtly tongue and teeth,
Having on the lovely earth
A girl's faith in great passion,
A tryst among young birches,
O Jesus Christ, and a kiss.
For an earthly tare, futile,
By God, how great is man's pride,
To build a sinful burden,
A strange place for vanity.
Busy sprout, no proud passage,
Ponder your time, be not proud.

THE COAL-TIT

Go, bird of no pretensions,
Fly aloft, treble-voiced tit,
Dear the one at one with me,
From the south to my sweetheart.

Make for Meirion, flawless gift,
Bright song in May's young thorntrees.
Swift your flight bridging a hedge,
Rider of full-branched birches.
Soon-wearied wing, smooth grey bill,
You're a bird of four colours,
Green and blue, watchful servant,
White and black, tending to leaves,
Companion to young people,
Though tiny, shaper of tunes.

Master of secret missions,
You are quick, small grey-cheeked bird :
Dart like the wind, a wild rush,
To my gold dear in Meirion ;
Labour, lord of sweet language,
Your wings above the dark woods.
Greet that comely complexion :
Bid Dafydd's wife a good-day.

My sweetheart, she : for my sake,
Gold her chamber, beseech her,
White wave's hue of Merioneth,
Not to enter, night or day,
My second soul, thick gold thatch,
Sweet girl, the bed of Eiddig.

This too, squire, brisk and noble,
Bard of trees the hawk forsakes,
Lucky possessor of two
Lean legs, farers through forests,
Bold you must be, I'm eager,
Be bold this once to my love.

Tell her, bird, diligent bard,
Woods' seer in time of torment,
That I with a song of love

Am in Deheubarth, brother,
In my heart seven sorrows,
Shaft of yearning for her sake.

Since I've not seen, clear-voiced bird,
Bright wall and brilliant image —
Plead my praise that will conquer —
This month, a marvel I live.

LAMENT FOR LLEUCU LLWYD

For gay bard, barren summer,
Barren the world for a bard.
I was stripped bare, grief's comrade,
For choosing this month to tryst.
Today in Gwynedd remains
No moon, no light, no colour,
Since they placed, sorry welcome,
Beauty's moon in the hard ground.

Fair girl in the chest of oak,
I'm bent on wrath, you left me.
Lovely form, Gwynedd's candle,
Though you are closed in the grave,
Arise, come up, my dearest,
Open the dark door of earth,
Refuse the long bed of sand,
And come to face me, maiden.
Here is, heavy cost of grief,
Above your grave, sun's beauty,
A sad-faced man without you,
Llywelyn, bell of your praise.
Wailing bard, I am walking
A foul world, fierce passion's slave.
Dear one, whose worth grew daily,

Yesterday over your grave
I let tears fall in torrents
Like a rope across my cheeks.

But you, mute girl's fair image,
From the pit made no reply.
Sadly silent, lacking love,
You promised, speechless maiden,
Mild your manner, silk-shrouded,
To stay for me, fair bright girl,
Till I came, I know the truth,
Strong safeguard, from the southland.
I heard nothing, straight-spoken,
But the truth, slim silent girl,
Measure of maidens, Indeg,
Before this, from your sweet mouth.
Hard blow, why care where's my home,
You broke faith, and it grieves me.

You are, my cywydd is false,
Truthful, words sweetly spoken :
It's I, grief's spilled-out language,
Who lie in sad harmonies ;
I'm lying, skimping prayer,
Lying the words I have cried.
I will leave Gwynedd today,
What care I where, bright beauty,
My fine flowering sweetheart :
If you lived, by God, I'd stay !
Where shall I, what care I where,
See you, fair moon, pale blossom,
On Mount, Ovid's passion spurned,
Olivet, radiant maiden ?
You've secured my place surely,
Lleucu, fair wave's comely hue,
Beautiful bright-skinned maiden,
Asleep too long under stone.

Rise to finish the feasting,
See if you thirst for some mead,
Come to your bard, whose laughter
Has long ended, golden crown.
Come, with your cheeks of foxgloves,
Up from the earth's dreary house.
A wayward trail the footprints,
No need to lie, my feet leave,
In faltering from passion
About your house, Lleucu Llwyd.
All the words, Gwynedd's lantern,
That I have sung, face of snow,
Three sighs of grief, gold-ringed hand,
Lleucu, praised you, my precious.
With these lips, skilled in praising,
What I'll sing, life-long, in praise,
My dear, foam's hue on rivers,
My love, will be your lament.

Lucid, sweet-spoken Lleucu,
My sweetheart's legacy was :
Her soul, Merioneth's treasure,
To God the Father, true vow ;
Her slender, fine flour's colour,
Body to sanctified soil ;
Girl mourned far, flour-white favour,
World's wealth to the proud dark man ;
And yearning, a song of grief,
This legacy she left me.

Two equal gifts, sad custom,
Pretty Lleucu, snow-spray's hue,
Earth and stone, bitter grief's gem,
Cover her cheeks, and oakwood.
Ah God, so heavy's the grave,
The earth on beauty's mistress.

Ah God, a coffin holds you,
Between us a house of stone,
Church chancel and stone curtain
And earth's weight and gown of wood.
Ah God, fair girl of Pennal,
A nightmare, buried your brow.
Hard lock of oak, bitter grief,
And earth, your brows were lovely,
And heavy door, heavy clasp,
And the land's floor between us,
A firm wall, a hard black lock,
A latch — farewell, my Lleucu.

THE SNOW

Sad harvest of high spirits,
These are my thoughts, I am old,
While snow through January
Locks the lid on Gwynedd's land,
Frozen life's force, then arrive
Small writs, urging my leaving :
If they stay atop the hill,
White snowfalls will not let me.

This plague impedes all vigour,
As Mary knows, pallid walls,
Frown worse than the shire's sheriff,
Round mantle of fallow moors,
Fierce stream that festers the face,
Lime-white curtain of canvas.
Long it's bombarded each spot,
Blobs of sky, mount of fodder,
Sign of wrath, weir of rush-tips,
Cold wax on heather and rocks,
Fine snow of mist and hoarfrost,

I

Winnowing sheet, no path bare,
Since the plug, pale appearance,
Was pulled from the pit of salt,
To salt with snow the foul path,
Broad earth's flooring, huge larder.
Cold came on each grove's fullness,
Large crop, like a maiden's skin.
Enduring it's no delight,
Fine flour of heaven's elders.
If rain comes where it's roosted,
Pale-bellied, burdened earth's bane,
Sharp from the sky, here's warning,
Cardigan's flood holds me back ;
Unlikely I'll ford Dyfi,
The torrent stopped stags today.

I'm no wretched wanderer,
No need to leave till summer
The place that's been paradise,
The courts so fair and comely.
Glowing words the sons of Meurig,
Lord of song's wall, offer me ;
From Hywel's house, noble line,
I go to Meurig's, no wastrel ;
My task, while I'm with my lords,
Will be, I'm their old uncle,
To read law, need's ready words,
And *Brut*, old tale of Britain,
To wear each man's gleaming hand's
Splendid gifts, green to please me,
Loudly mock the maddened mob,
How they roar, dunghill minstrels,
Onrush like that which robbed me,
Swiftly compare Lleucu Llwyd
To lovely garden roses,
Kind Mary, or the fair sun.
Delight for a thin, frail man,

A fine time comes on Sunday,
Listening after Christmas
To the cooks slicing the meat,
Din of greyhounds, there's no doubt,
Shaggy-haired, from their shackles,
Quick fiddle and bagpipe blent,
Blending of voices nightly,
And sanctus bells and laughter
And hailing men to have wine.
My prayer, my handsome lords,
My hearts, they do not leave me,
Old uncle to gay nephews,
Alone to battle the plague.
A building, there I'll linger,
Between their houses I'll have,
Amidst the place of my praise,
Talk of wine, Cae Gwrgenau.
They gave a rousing banquet,
I'm no older than them both.

Gruffudd Gryg

THE APRIL MOON

April moon, hideous hue,
Mournful is your expression,
Glassy coin, silver-coated,
Stark moon, men would think you slain.
Each day your dejected hue
You alter, face of anger,
Blushing before rushing winds,
Blue-grey before rain rages.
Pallid crust, sorry circle,
I languish, are you in love ?

Sky-clout, your silence be praised,
Are you unwell, wench ?   Hear me :
Which of your tribe, troubled tale,
Have you lost, flinty florin ?
There's no day, mirror's semblance,
Icy cheeks, you do not heave,
Oppression's edge, a thousand
Of your sighs, and sometimes three.
Each sigh, strong expiration,
Would shatter a stone in three.
Each night, wan and warm, awry,
Wretched wheel, you spend weeping,
Errant erratic planet,
A plate, a tear-dripping vent,
How is it you weep in air,
Worn page, thin, pale, and crumpled ?

You broke your bond with Saint James,
Land of rain, you're dishonoured.
You hurled me to Harry's shore,
Still hold me, my opponent.

122

Unless James use, most precious,
Force, my lad Jenkin and I,
We can, though we swam the sky,
Not come home, sorry hindrance.
Sad is the lord who saw you,
I've paid for your rage, by God.
You wrenched me, often wretched,
Cold flood-path, off a fair course :
Wheel winding tide's ebb and flow,
Third of a worn stone handmill,
Dark covert, strong deceiver,
Ball flaming with Michael's fire,
Flat stone of the seething sky,
Wide breadth of a sharp spindle,
You were a dimming lantern,
A grey stone eye of deluge,
Windy Troy, far-sailing hull,
Sky's cairn, bare crown of April,
Cold weather's twirling taper,
Lead buckler of pale bare spring,
Deep-set tempestuous cauldron,
You arrive, and I'm driven wild.
You've taught clouds to crowd round me,
Now come down, rain's coverlid :
Let another, foul colour,
Frigid moon, assume your place.

Worthless cold sky of April,
I am pledged, without a doubt,
Hate for a lad has never
Fashioned a worse end to spring.
Sign of an ill-starred journey,
Fresh shame to spring, frigid wind.
Choicest month, with cheeks glowing,
Come with the sun, summer's ray,
Bring one ship a fair true course
Safe from cold skies in April.

May, magic Kai, rising woods,
Because I'll sing your praises,
Bring me, fair month, a straight road,
Bring to Saint James his bounty.
No unlovely April, calm.
May moon, pilot your poet.

LAMENT FOR RHYS AP TUDUR

Gwynedd is like, they're saying,
From frenzy, sad if it's true,
Fiddle and bell, man's groaning,
Many pounds in price, and harp :
The fiddle that kept strict time,
Loved to play songs of Jesus,
Harsh will be, day after day,
Its playing, the strings lacking ;
The harp of golden lineage,
Night and day a nightingale,
Lacking men's hands, proper pledge,
Lacking song, lacking fingers,
Like a ploughbeam its carved wood,
Will give, I think, no pleasure ;
Each matin bell, ill fortune,
From the close of churchly men,
If its chain-rope were broken
And its strong prophetic tongue,
None would love, sounding edges,
Its peal in pulpit and choir.

And thus, praise worthy of mead,
For its vintage does Gwynedd
Lack Môn's lord, lack frequent song,
Lack bells, lack the shrine's jewel,
Lack the Lord's hand, lack a tongue,

Lack harp-song, lack good fortune,
Lack feasting, lack diversion,
Lack good lord Rhys, lack kind gifts,
Lack bright beauty, lack dawnlight,
Lack grace, lack honour, lack all,
Lack more honour, high floodtide,
From Richard, an eagle's shield,
Fortune's heart, pillar of gold,
King, who spread fields with Angles.

Were not his bright deeds, Môn's praise,
And his eyes like an eagle's ?
He paid heed to my sorrow,
Sweet lord, was his fee not fair ?
Did he not show, fine vintage,
Wisdom at the court of France ?
Was he not merry, modest,
This Elffin, poured wine, brave Rhys ?
Is not Gwynedd, grand my style,
Empty for a dark eagle,
For Rhys, lad of grim ruin,
Gold chain, Tudur's line, sword's edge,
True keeper, and it grieves me,
War's victor, of Snowdon's stags ?

There is in Gwynedd, wrath's face,
Men say, unless God save us,
No strength, no safety for us,
No banquets, no great nobles,
No compact of true passion,
No pursuit of song, no art,
No wooing of pure maidens,
No loving a girl, no mead,
No tree-ringed tryst with a dear,
No birds in woodland birches,
No merry hillside, no twigs,
No delight, except Eiddig's.

Gwynedd, most honoured dwelling,
Hear this and hope for my praise,
Witness my oath, wine-blest face,
Wrath's word, to your hand, Gwynedd,
From anger, my grief's anguish,
Pain and pledge, you'll have no more,
Twenty wails for war's master,
Lord of praise, a man like him.

DAFYDD'S WOUNDS

A marvel is poor Dafydd,
Son of Gwilym, faultless man,
A bold lad, grief's bedfellow,
Weakened by a hundred wounds.
And still the wearisome lad
Toys with song, and swoons captive.
Lengthy, weak work, his moaning,
God's mother, it is, says he,
Sad ruin for a Welshman ;
It's strange that he's still alive.

In all quarters, quaking cheek,
Mary hears how he suffers.
Pains plentiful as stars are
Devouring Dafydd's body.
It grieves me if bitter pains
Afflict the master poet :
Pain not of clashing armies,
Not plague pain, languishing pain,
Pain not of back, much burdened,
Not sharp pain, but sickliness,
Pain not frequent, not fevered,
Not forceful, but feeble pain.

Weapons, lord of woven song,
Are deep within his bosom.
It is ten years to the day
Dafydd has said, fine singing,
Nearly a hundred weapons
Were in him, buffets of steel,
Arrows, vexing frustrations,
That were piercing him with pain.
A mighty weakness he suffered,
So men thought, with pains like these.

A big lie, deceitful bard,
Dafydd spoke in his folly.
Were it Arthur, mighty wall,
Swift to assault an army,
The truth is, if all those pains
Hurt in a hundred places,
The wars he waged were savage,
Truth is he'd not live a month,
Much less then, the lad's slender,
Love's servant, frail as he is.
It grieves me : were he wounded
With a spear by one from Môn,
With his ringed hand on his lance,
Keenly piercing his bosom,
Not a long hour of morning
Would he live, his colour's poor,
Much less, no pleasant notion,
Swooning with so many wounds.

Sadness is the death of him,
Weapons have killed his colour.
By my faith, this clever lad,
For all his pride and boasting,
A shrewd foreigner could cause
Grief, with a stiff reed arrow.
He's in danger, sorely tried,
Of death from Morfudd's weapons !

THE FICKLE GIRL

Maiden of noble breeding
In the midst of mead and wine,
You are well-mannered, well-made,
And you, fair one, are fickle.
What warrants being fickle
When our compact's lasted long ?

Though you're well-born and clever
And have riches in your grasp,
Be not proud, my lime-white girl,
You should not, it's not fitting ;
It's less likely I'll go to
The proud than the meek who'll come.
The slanders of noble suitors,
Trust them not, until you see ;
Do not frown, lest you be scorned,
Snowdrift hue, and refuse me.

If contrite for loving me,
What's been, slim girl, is buried,
Since, clever smooth-spoken dear,
Cold care, you love another :
May God, Saints Non and David,
Let him gladly have your heart,
And for me, precious jewel,
What God wills, my lovely dear.
Do not make me, in anger,
Point a finger at your friend.

There was a day, in fine style,
Placid gem, when you listened,
Many a kiss and greeting,
Many a nod, noble girl,
Many a sign, gold-haired moon,

And many trysts on hillsides,
Birch chaplets under birches,
And many a clasp of hands,
And now am I, she's untrue,
By Saint Dwyn, not acknowledged.

You've been vexed with one you loved,
It grieves me, how you've spoken.
Be prudent, sweet, curb your wrath,
Love God, redeem your promise.
Beware of being judged a
Bitter fraud, player at dice :
Though winning for the moment,
Wretched is greed, the world turns ;
It could be, lime-white beauty,
The world will turn on the proud.
If you, fine-looking maiden,
Follow after fickleness,
Beware, girl, though they greet you,
The course that one man once took
Who freed the ears before he,
Long he scowled, had seized the horns.

Since before you know you're wrong,
Grave word, you choose another,
Farewell, my slender sweetheart,
Now there's nothing else for me ;
Farewell, deceitful lover,
I'll bury, dear, what has been.

THE YEW-TREE

For the best of lads, yew-tree,
By the wall of Ystrad Fflur,
May God bless you, bliss of trees,

Grown as a home for Dafydd.
Saintly Dafydd foresaw you
Before your growth as a shield ;
Dafydd, when you were full-grown,
Honoured, even from boyhood,
You as a green-leaved bower,
A home, and each leafy grove,
Fort shielding the dead from storm
As once did woodland branches.

Beneath you there is silence,
A close grave, not as I'd choose,
Beehive of swarming angels,
A brave man, laid in the grave,
And skill of song, well-measured,
And Dyddgu grieves that he's dumb.
He made her a green dwelling,
A lavish growth, while he lived ;
Now must you, chosen branches,
Be straight and fair for this lord.
His grave is gently tended,
Good yew trivet like an aunt.

Obey, do not grow crooked,
Yew-tree, stay over the grave.
No goats will taint or tear you,
Growing at your father's foot,
Nor fire burn you, fierce greeting,
Nor carpenter cut, love wound,
Nor cobbler peel, while men live,
The cover from your dwelling.
No fuel seekers, no churl
Will chop, their hearts are timid,
With an axe, green your burden,
At your base for fear of blame,
Roof of leaves, room most pleasant,
God safeguard your miracles.

CHRIST THE KING

Who's the Man commands the crown ?
Fair God, pierced is His bosom,
Christ, worthy king of heaven,
Pure body of bread and wine.
It's He our flowing language
Should name as both One and Three ;
Father and Son offered up
And faithful Holy Spirit ;
You're our Lord above all lords,
Our bulwark, and our Father.

He's surely the best of men,
A good man was His baptist ;
Good the fair, faultless maiden
Who nourished Him as her son,
Bearing a while deep sorrow
Before His pain for the world.
The Jewish people wholly
Cast scorn upon His five wounds ;
They bound about His forehead
A crown of a hundred thorns,
And every thorn was bleeding,
Torn the skull of Mary's son ;
His flesh was a mass of wounds
And pierced, and His breast bleeding ;
And wrenched He was, life over,
Speedily down from the cross.
For Christ, then, there was mourning,
Hastily placed in the grave ;
And afterwards four foemen
Kept watch over holy God.
Joyful were men of His land,
Mary ! mighty His rising ;
And all of us, as one flock,

We can rejoice for ever.
Judas, He'd not deserved it,
Bears the blame for selling Him ;
A man unblessed was Judas
When he sold, for gain, this Man.

Because His hands knew torment,
Because He rose from the grave,
Let us ask our God on high,
There, where He bought us heaven,
Ask the Father, dear saviour,
Jesus is called full of grace,
Watch over us, bring all men,
Our refuge, home to heaven.

Iolo Goch

SIR HYWEL OF THE AXE

Have any seen what I see
At night, and I do rightly,
When I, never such torment,
Am sleeping an old man's sleep ?
What I see first is truly
A fair large fort by the sea,
A fine masterful castle,
Men on the walks, and a wall,
Blue sea by a stone rampart,
Waves about a black keep's womb,
And tune of flutes and bagpipes,
Lively lord, noteworthy man,
Maidens, no lack of beauty,
Weaving beautiful bright silk,
Proud men playing, in great hall,
Draughts and chess at the dais,
A grizzled man, fierce-tempered,
Twrch Trwyd of war, giving wine
In a gilded gold goblet
From his hand into my hand,
Lovely banner, long and black,
Atop this good knight's tower,
Three beautiful white flowers
Shaped the same, with silver leaves.

Strange that there's not an elder
In Gwynedd, land of great feasts,
Who's capable of knowing
If I may be where I would.
'A proud man,' says one, 'you are,
Here below, in your dreaming.

The splendid wall that you see,
The good dwelling you'd come to,
The bright fort on rocky heights,
Red stone at the croft's border,
Is Cricieth, well constructed,
An ancient building it is.
The grey spear-splintering man's
Hywel, hurler of lightning,
Warlord at need, Sir Hywel,
And his golden-girdled wife ;
And her fair-complexioned maids,
All twelve of them, were weaving
Beautiful bright-coloured silk,
Fine glass letting in sunlight.
When you saw, in your vision,
A banner, fine its design,
Sir Hywel's pennon it is :
By Beuno, in his banner
Three fleur-de-lys, field iris,
On sable, no lack of pomp.'

The son of red-speared Gruffudd
Is so made he makes for foes,
Whetting his spear in their blood,
Savage, gold-footed chieftain,
Carver of war, clear red H,
Quick to the fray, red-shielded,
Tusks of a terrible boar,
The old bone that we needed.
When greed's reward, the bridle,
Was put on the king of France,
He played barber like Geraint
With sword and spear, battle's weight,
With his hand and his deftness
Shaving off both heads and beards,
Soaking, as quick as he could,
Feet with blood, grief to many.

Dear he'll be to fair Einiort,
Many his bards, praised his board.
He's warden, eighteen-tined stag,
Steward of the strong fortress,
Bold knight, the garrison's guard,
Long will he guard this region.
He'll guard those in his strong seat,
Guard the keep, he's worth armies,
Guard two borders, field-warden,
Guard two lands, army, and fame,
Guard the sea-bull and seastrand,
Guard the tide, guard homes, guard ground,
Guard all lands, guard the tower,
Guard the fort : here's to his health !

SYCHARTH

Twice I have pledged this to you,
Fair pledge, pledging a journey.
Let each, as much as he may,
Redeem the pledge he pledges.
A pilgrimage, faith's blessing,
Occasion most dear to me,
I'll make, mine's a true promise,
For my good to Owain's court.
There unswervingly I'll go,
No trouble, there I'll settle
To have a life of honour
With him, welcome interchanged.

He can, my lord most royal,
Chief of bards, welcome the weak.
I hear he's good, no secret,
Blameless journey, to the old.

K

To his court in haste I'll go,
The two hundred best worthies,
A baron's court, high manners,
With many bards, a fine life,
Lord of great Powys, Maig's land,
The one whom true hope longs for.
Look at its form and fashion,
Moated with water's gold round,
Fine manor, bridge on the moat,
A hundred-pack-wide portal.
In couples, a coupled work,
Each of the couples coupled,
Patrick's belfry, fruit of France,
Westminster's smooth-linked cloister.
Clasped the same is each corner,
Gold sanctum, a perfect whole.

Bands in the hillside above
Side by side like a dungeon
And each, like a knot tied tight,
Interlocked with the other.
Nine-fold mould, eighteen chambers,
Green hilltop, fine-timbered house.
On four marvellous pillars
Close to heaven is his hall.
On each firm wooden pillar
A loft on the sturdy croft,
And the four lofts, delightful,
Are linked, there the minstrels sleep,
Four splendid lofts, converted,
A fine well-filled nest, to eight.
Tile roofs on the tall houses,
Chimneys that cannot nurse smoke,
Nine halls in matching pattern,
And nine wardrobes in each one,
Fine shops with comely contents,
Well-stocked shop like London's Cheap.

Cross-tipped church, clean lime-white walls,
Chapels and fair glass windows.

Each side full, each house at court,
Orchard, vineyard, white fortress ;
The master's rabbit warren ;
Ploughs and strong steeds of great fame ;
Near the court, even finer,
The deer park within that field ;
Fresh green meadows and hayfields ;
Neatly enclosed rows of grain ;
Fine mill on smooth-flowing stream ;
Dove-cot, a bright stone tower ;
A fish-pond, enclosed and deep,
Where nets are cast when need be,
Abounding, no argument,
In pike and splendid whiting ;
His land a board where birds dwell,
Peacocks, high-stepping herons.

His serfs do their proper work,
Fill the needs of the region,
Bringing Shrewsbury's new beer,
Spirits, the first-brewed bragget,
All drinks, white bread and wine,
His meat, fire for his kitchen.
Tent of bards from all regions,
All welcomed there, every day.
The best wife among women,
I'm blest by her wine and mead,
A knightly line's bright daughter,
Proud hostess of royal blood.
His children come, two by two,
A fine nestful of princes.

Seldom has there been seen there
Either a latch or a lock,

Or someone playing porter,
No lack of bountiful gifts,
No need, no hunger, no shame,
No one is parched at Sycharth.
The best Welshman, bold leader,
Owns this land, Pywer Lew's line,
Slim strong man, the land's finest,
And owns this court, place to praise.

THE PLOUGHMAN

When, on their day of freedom,
All people of Christendom,
In God's presence, Lord most loved,
Bold words, disclose their doings,
On top of, where all are judged,
Mount Olivet the mighty,
Cheerful will be, glad story,
The ploughman, plodder of fields.
If he gave, God is lavish,
Offering and tithes to God,
Then a good upright spirit
He'll show God, deserving grace.

Easily may the ploughman
Of fine dales trust the Lord God :
Alms, through faith strictly followed,
Lodging, he'll deny to none ;
He'll pass on nothing but ploughs,
He does not care for quarrels ;
He wants no part of warfare,
He'll press no one for what's his ;
He'll not treat us too harshly,
He'll drive no unjust demands ;
It is his role to suffer ;
Without him, no life or world.

He finds it far more pleasant
I know, in his quiet way,
To hold, no need to blame him,
The curving plough and the goad,
Than to be a plunderer,
Like Arthur, downing towers.
We'd lack without his labour
Christ's sacrifice, food of faith.
Neither pope nor emperor
Possesses life without him,
Nor merry king who freely
Pours out wine, nor living man.

The Elucidarium,
Sound old book, said it clearly :
'Blessed is he, from boyhood,
Who holds a plough with his hands.'
Cradle that splits the soft broom,
Creel skilled in slicing meadows,
A precious thing, gladly praised,
Crane opening fine furrows,
Creel of the fertile wild earth,
Coulter-carrying framework,
Gander of untamed acres,
With sure skill supplying grain,
Fetching crops from fertile soil,
A fine colt chewing ploughland.
It likes its knife and table
And its food under its thigh.
Reluctant to ride pebbles,
It flays earth, its leg in front.
Its head stays busy on the
Street beneath the oxen's feet.
It sings its hymn-tune often,
Loves chasing after the chain,
Shatters roots in the valley
Stretching its unbending neck,

A train-bearer, not feeble,
Earth-scattering wooden leg.

Hugh the Strong, king of many,
Who rewarded song with wine,
Emperor of land and sea,
Constantinople's keeper,
Put his hand, when defeated,
To a splendid strong-beamed plough.
A healthy lord, he never,
Striker in battle, sought bread,
Except, good was his teacher,
By his own labour, land's bard,
Thus showing, gifted eagle,
To humble men and to proud
That one craft, these words are true,
Ranks highest with the Father,
A sign that it will triumph,
Ploughing — it is wisdom's way.

Where there's belief and baptism
And all men maintain the faith,
God's hand is, the best of men,
Mary's hand's on each ploughman.

PORTRAIT OF A MAIDEN

I love, she's tender-hearted,
Rowan-berried, coral cheeks.
Proud sweetheart, she poured out mead,
Kind girl of Tegfedd's castle.
Glowing-cheeked flawless branch,
Spray of foaming fresh water,
Flourishing firm white hemlock,
Straight-bodied, slander-shy dear,

Skin fair as sunlit tower,
Rush body no man has known,
Hue of light snow on grey stone,
Gleam of rock-rippled water,
She made me ache, many moans,
Meek red-checked branch of Llywy.
Moon's face, hue of new year's snow,
She's mild and fair, a dawnlight.

Fine this untamed maiden's looks
And her taste, form of Iseult :
Beautiful, well was she made,
Not bashful, by Saint David ;
Forehead's wrought gold well-moulded,
Primrose hair, a golden hill ;
Hue of Eigr, rich radiant prize,
Dark slim brow, Mary's image ;
Eye like a splendid crown's gem,
Seems a stone of the Tiboeth ;
Full smile, rimed gossamer's hue,
Dainty nose, faint its sneezes ;
Sweet little teeth, a pretty
Delightful lip that sips wine ;
Long throat, a fair flowering,
Swan-like, shapely, well-rounded ;
Thumb that numbers her prayerbeads,
Arm, and apple-ripe bosom ;
Slender hand of a glove's hue,
Long dirk, soft pretty fingers,
With pinkish nails upon them,
And there, a circle of gold ;
Goddess' flank, smooth and lovely,
A noble estate's rich chain ;
Round leg, snowy hilltrail's hue,
Pale beneath skirt of scarlet ;
Below fur fringe, slim ankle,
A shapely white foot, if short.

If a finger's crooked quickly
Before her, curved pebble eye,
White-nailed rush, frail miracle,
She sways like ears of barley.
Girl of fair snow, smooth-templed,
White border on fine gold sleeves,
Blessed is she, pale her cheek,
She wears, my red-lipped maiden,
A white head-dress, none so wise,
Fair pennon, pure-browed peahen.
Who could, though an architect,
Paint with lime her appearance ?

God made her, the Son's project,
By Peter, for His Son's sake.
I've piled up song, feeble point,
Love's brush, am I not brash to
Hope I'll (why's she been lavish ?)
Sleep with my sly-glancing girl ?

THE SHIP

Hard for me, one friendly word
Of the ship, its deck's frigid,
Saddle of booming billows,
Jailhouse above bitter brew,
Black couch in pale cold fury,
Bright cider painfully cold.
No chance, fiend's calving frenzy,
Of welcome on the ship's deck.
Much punishment, it pained me
To live in it, thin frail thing.

She would rock, faulty creature,
On her side, quivering cold.

God's wrath to me, seas' cheesehouse,
Cramped castle, seafarers' chest.
She's a thin-staved false-steering
Foul Noah's ark of a ship.
Sooty oak, sharp her furrow,
Spry old cow, round-walled, pale-clad,
Cart of coal, not a clean court,
Her sail coarse cloth, wide open,
High-nosed hag, scabby-lipped boards,
Wide-nostrilled, rope-reined saddle,
New moon, broad pan for kneading,
She's clumsy as an old churn,
Swift tower, bulky shadow,
Stiff screen seven cubits high,
Swift-leaping sea-splashing mare,
Bowl unsteadily bouncing,
Scabby crab-bowelled jailhouse,
Broad mare, seen as far as France.
She'd make a face with seaweed,
Sea-cat, teeth under her breast.
More than a mark her rental,
Bent basket amidst green cork.
She has filth, oath of Arthur,
In her cracks like stone wall.

So, fine renunciation,
I'll go no more to my doom,
Thirsty vessel, bleak, cold, black,
An old sea-going cupboard.
Dull slut, she has been in Greece,
Broad anchorage, black, frigid.
Slow-sailing sty of a sow,
Brittle, mast-bristling vessel,
Broad sled for gritty gravel,
She'd leap furrows, poor cold mare,
Foul wagon's belly, ill-famed,
Cold snake like Sir Fulke's stallion.

Thick-foaming yeast comes pouring,
Salt negress, stone-bellied snake,
Harrow smoothing the ocean,
Hind of the ridges of sea.

Often, on the cold border,
When the wild sea-tides would flow,
I gave greeting, festive hour,
Golden helm, to the Cilmael,
Where Rhys was, Lazarus' court,
Robert's son, famous kinsman.
There I'd have, generous gift,
A drink of his gold bragget.
It's there, praiseworthy refuge,
I'd be were I where I'd be.

BARD AND BEARD

Is it you, beard, scared away
The girl who kindly kissed me ?
You are too thickly planted,
A great harvest on my chin.
Black and sharp, harsh and Irish,
When I gaze into my glass,
My complexion has become,
Chinful of grain, all hairy.

However completely cut,
However closely shaven,
No smoother, all can see it,
Than a beer-hued coarse fish-tail.
The fair girl liked but little
My mouth, because of my beard ;
Always rough was the jaw's edge,
More bruising bristles daily.

A hag would find them helpful,
Troop of toothless carding combs.
On my face, so they tell me,
Stuff with a thousand small teeth.
It's a slowpoke hedgehog's coat,
Chin's burden, like muzzle,
Harsh-stinging points of holly,
Goads of steel scaring a girl.

Old roebuck's hair, where's your source ?
You are a crop of gorse-shoots.
Sharp and strong is every hair,
Sticking a girl, stiff heather,
Resembling, so harsh they grow,
A thousand thistle feathers.
You are like frozen stubble,
Seamless stiff-tipped arrow quills.
Go away ! Prevent dishonour,
Chin's thatch, like a horse's mane.

Should my chin begin ageing,
With hot water, out it comes !

LAMENT FOR DAFYDD AP GWILYM

CYWYDD   An enchantment, Dafydd's life,
Blithe man, would it were longer,
Rhyme intertwined, fine passion,
Gwilym Gam's son, knot of song.
He shaped praise in strict pattern,
A good practice in a man.
Prepared am I, I'll fashion
A lament for love of him.
The counties' gem and their crest
And the land's brooch and beauty,

The mould and means of pleasure,
Turning me loose for fair gifts,
Hawk of Deheubarth's daughters,
Without him, what's left is chaff.
The cywydd of each sweet singer,
Because he's gone, moans in grief.

BARD

And you, hound, quiet, cywydd !
Life's not good, will not last long.
While Dafydd lived, skilled in song,
You were an honoured pastime ;
And therefore, now that he's gone,
To ask for you's not fitting.
Let songs woven of couplets
Be tossed away to the loft.
He has gone, words' architect ;
In life, all men's instructor.
Fearful my sad stricken moan,
The one art's wondrous master,
And tiler of love for a girl,
And harp of court and household,
Bursar of bards and their fame,
Trident of test and trial,
And wretched without restraint,
Bold despoiling a maiden,
Roofbeam of bards, world's sorrow,
He will never rise again.
Strong master, bright-voiced and bold,
Monarch, he's gone to heaven.

Gruffudd Llwyd

MORGANNWG

Fair sun, upon my errand
Run now, for you're daylight's wheel,
The fairest planet that runs,
Fair sun, in God's possession.

Sunday's source, excellent light,
On a long trail you travel
From east, fair weather's sky-road,
Finest of colours, to west.
Fullness of grace surrounds you,
Shining you are on both sides,
Your lustre, by God above,
The whole world's length it stretches.
Splendid sun, from your fair hue
The moon derived its colour,
Supreme rule, oval rowel,
Round wheel, great your gift and grace.
Bright-complexioned gem of light,
You are the daylight's empress.

Most noble planet I love,
Blesséd the length of summer
Are you above, flawless day,
All of Morgannwg daily,
Generous, strong wise people,
From Gwent, where the men are good,
To, there you know how to fly,
Glyn Nydd, fair royal region.
For my sake, sun, mild curtain,
Keep from the fair land of wine
Too much rain, bridges' danger,
Too much frost, and too much wind,

147

Baleful stars, and harsh fury
Through the trees, and lasting snow,
And whirlwind's far-faring force,
And rime in early April.
Display, day's pitch of splendour,
Morgannwg's banner each day,
And after noon, light's fullness,
Come and visit by my side.
Though below the sky tonight,
Thick veil, in western regions,
Broad image, splendid dwelling,
Come back once more in the east :
Rise for me now, truly mindful,
In heaven's height before prime.

Go on my errand, carry
With you to Morgannwg's men
Fine days, dwelling-place of love,
From me, and bring my greeting.
Turn, no need to command you,
About the great whitewashed halls ;
Wondrous, God's gift, your story,
Send through the glass beams of light.
Seek out each place of pleasure,
Meadow and wood, where there's mead,
Each mansion, fair is your range,
And every glade and orchard.

What sort of land ?   A radiance.
Poets call it Paradise.
Corner opposite Cornwall,
It's my court of wine and mead.
Place where many find pleasure,
Place of good households and wine,
Place resounding with welcome,
Place of proud lads and pure maids,
Place of poet's ease, gay crowds,

Look on, bright lovely daylight,
The best bards truly ask it,
A fine woman in white fur.

I send, with fair weather's lord,
Fine fcasts, this land a title,
In a true lover's language,
'Countess, and Queen of all lands.'
Were faith to all forbidding
Any the freedom to give,
In Morgannwg, rich language,
No one could ever say no.
If banned to a lively bard
Were the world, as an outcast,
He'd have, no frown would appear,
Provision in Morgannwg !

Poems of Unknown or Uncertain Authorship

THE SNOW

No sleep, no leaving my house :
This causes me discomfort.
No world, no ford, no hillside,
Nowhere clear, no land today.
No girl's promise will lure me
Out of my house into snow.
A plague, these plumes cling on clothes
As if they played at dragon.
My clothing is my excuse :
It looks much like a miller's.
Isn't it true, after New Year's,
Everyone's dressed in ermine ?
In the first month of the year
God's busy making hermits.

To the dark ground round about
God has given a whitewash :
No woodland not clad in white,
No bush without a blanket,
Fine flour the fur on each branch,
Sky's flour like April flowers,
Cold white veil on the greenwood,
Load of lime bowing the trees,
Apparition of wheat flour,
Level land's coat of metal.
Cold gravel's spread on ploughed ground,
Earth's skin thick-caked with tallow,
Foam in too thick a shower,
Fleece bigger than a man's fist.

Stinging through Gwynedd they came,
White they are, bees from heaven.

Where does God start such a plague ?
What place stores saints' goose-feathers ?
Twin brother to piled-up husks,
Stoat-shirted, strides the heather.
The dust has turned to snowdrift
Where once were small paths and praise.
Who knows in January
What sort of mob's spitting down ?
Heaven's white angels, no less,
Are busy with their building.

See how the board's been pulled from
The bottom of the flour loft.
Silver dress of ice this while,
The world's coldest quicksilver,
Cold cloak, whose stay makes sorry,
Cement of hill, ditch, and dale,
Steel skirt binding earth's belly,
Slab greater than the sea's grave,
A huge bulk's on my region,
A pale wall from sea to sea.
The earth from its four corners
Has had its whole brain laid bare.

Where's it from, this cold white plate ?
Magic plaster, who'll stop it ?
Who is there dares to shame it ?
It's lead on cloaks.   Where's the rain ?

THE GROVE OF BROOM

Her form and hue are finer
Than a countess' gown of gold.
Two things I'll say : sad is one
Who may not meet, not see her.

L

I've no freedom to venture
By day to a lovely moon ;
God forbids sleight, flawless face,
Beneath a wall at night-time.
No wood for a courtly lad
To keep tryst in green birches.
Long the wait, lovely image,
For summer without a tryst.

God to me and my darling
Gave a wood gowned in choice gold,
Twigs the equal of winter,
Fair leaves like a summerhouse.
There I'll fashion to charm her
A close of slender young broom,
As Merlin made, love's labour,
A glass house because of love.
In Dyfed they say that once
There was a secret curtain ;
Now beneath green branches,
My court is concealed like that.
If she'll come to my dwelling
She'll be countess in that court :
For her, I'll sing her praises,
There's life, soul's paradise,
Trees that have twined their branches,
Early leaves on tender twigs.

When May with his green livery
Comes to dignify young leaves,
Gold will flourish on the grove's
Fibres for him who holds it.
Lovely the grove and lavish
Grows the thick gold of its twigs.
God has, flawless the weaving,
Showered gold upon the twigs.

Let the girl be glad, the grove's
Paradise for a poet ;
The finest flowers I love,
These twigs are summer's hoarfrost.

There for me and my sweetheart
Is life, a fresh saffron field.
I've a house, a good dwelling
Made of Arabian gold.
Tent of the firmament's Lord,
Cloth of gold, the roof's speckled ;
A fair angel of heaven
Embroidered it for May's bed :
Gold gossamer, wondrous bees,
God's glow-worms, gems of sunlight.
What bliss, on the vine-clad hill
To have the young twigs gilded,
And the tips of bushes seen
Like the stars, golden bullion.

Thus have I, all one colour,
Flowers of May like small birds.
What a joyful thing it is,
The grove veiled like an angel !
I keep the grove and the glade,
Fine custom, for my sweetheart.
My bond's good, I'll not go from
The grove with its gold-speckled veil
Without, this summer, one tryst,
Gold-haired girl in the greenwood.
Let her come, where none part us,
Fair slim girl, beneath fresh broom.

THE STARS

God help me, girl, I must leave
The groves of May this springtime
To walk lovely slopes and woods,
My fair-haired girl, before I
May drink from the lake and see
Our bed beneath the birches.

Love is cruel, I clamour,
An assault transforming men.
I spent, I've sorrow enough,
Half the night, wretched journey,
Set on winning, kind sunlight,
Her kiss : I sought her consent.
By the high road I travelled,
Night-blinded on the bare moor.
A long trail last night, too dark,
Sad path to a slim maiden.
Many vile long-ridged pathways
Did I walk, a strong tall lad.
I stumbled through nine thickets,
And along bare ancient walls,
From there into a haven
Of fiends, the fellows of hate.
I passed from that green fastness
To bogs on the mountain's brow.
The black headland, this was hard,
Became darker to thwart me,
As if, after a battle,
I were pent up in a jail.
I crossed myself, no meek cry,
Too cold it was, too tangled.
I murmured, becoming numb,
A spell to ward off devils.
Bright scales wrapped in cloth of gold

Were sealed in a stone coffer,
And I am the next victim :
Till last night, thwarted the tryst,
Strong hissing, I had never
Been near that pestilent bog.

I vowed to visit, small price,
Llanddwyn, if I were rescued.
Mary's Son, sweet faith's treasure,
Never sleeps when He may save.
He saw how a bard suffered ;
God was gracious, lit for me
The zodiac's reed candles,
Fair downpour against distress.
Splendid and swiftly the stars
Appeared for us, night's cherries.
Lovely and bright was their light,
Sparks of seven saints' bonfires,
The unpraised moon's blazing plums,
The cold moon's cheerful berries.
Glands of the hideaway moon,
They are fair weather's kernels,
The moon's crop of gleaming nuts,
The Father's sun-bright pathways,
The omen of fine weather,
The eagle of each fair day.
The brilliant sun's flint mirror,
Glinting halfpennies of God,
Frozen rain's comely red gold,
Heaven's host's crupper jewels,
Sunlight hammers these nails in
The shield of sky, piercing deep.

Each pair's skilfully pounded,
The wide grey sky's clash of arms.
The swift wind will not shake them
From their peg-holes in the sky.

Far spread, wind cannot round them,
The vast sky's embers they are,
Chessboard and set of chessmen,
Brightly fashioned, on firm air,
Pins, I am fascinated,
In the head-dress of the sky.
Fair lights of praise like bright paths,
The sky's cover of clover,
Emblems on evening's pages,
Gilded frost, air's marigolds,
A hundred altar's candles
On the long stretch of the sky,
Fair-faceted beads of God,
Lacking a string, far scattered.

They revealed a vale and hill
To me, sunk deep in folly,
The roads to Môn, and my road ;
Pardon, Lord, my intention.
I came, not a wink of sleep,
At dawn to my love's dwelling.
I'll not boast of my hardship,
Just this, sweet generous girl :
Trying to use a good axe
To cut stone is no harder.

THE SWAN

Swan, on your beautiful lake,
As white-robed as an abbot,
You are, bird, the snowdrift's glow,
Angelic hue, round-footed.
Most solemn are your movements,
Handsome you are in your youth.
God has granted you for life
Lordship of Lake Yfaddon.

Two skills keep you from drowning,
Splendid gifts granted to you :
You are a master fisher,
Look at your skill on the lake,
And you are able to fly
Far above the high hilltop,
Glancing down, noble white bird,
To survey the earth's surface,
Scanning the lake-floor below,
Harvesting shoals like snowflakes.
You ride the waves superbly
To waylay fish from the deep.
Your fishing-rod, fair creature,
Is your long and lovely neck,
Keeper of the oval lake,
Breast the colour of seafoam.
You gleam on rippling water
In a crystal-coloured shirt,
A doublet, thousand lilies,
A splendid waistcoat, you wear,
A jacket of white roses,
Woodbine flowers for a gown.
You are the moon among birds,
White-cloaked, a cock of heaven.

Hear my complaint, good creature,
To you, and act as my aid.
There's a girl of noble birth,
A lovely queen, lives near you.
Make haste now, best of creatures,
Messenger, white under wings,
Swim as I ask, no delays,
And take the way to Cemais.
Keep this in mind, to ask for
The white moon of Tal-y-llyn.
The maiden to be greeted,
This, in my verse, is her name :

There's W, bold and fair,
D, Y, N are the others.
Go softly to her chamber,
Greet the exquisitely fair,
Reveal to her my sadness,
The depth of my suffering.
Bring me, she makes me angry,
Colourful creature, glad words.
God keep you from all evil,
Fair head, you'll have your reward.

THE TRYST

Cause of this stab in my side,
Girl I love, and have long loved,
Your colour God created,
Like the daisy is your brow.
Your red-gold is God's giving,
Your hair like a tongue of gold,
Your neck grows straight and slender,
Your breasts are full balls of yarn.
Your cheeks a charming scarlet,
Your brows, maid, are London black ;
Your eyes like two bright brooches,
Your nose, it's on a dear girl.
Your smile, five joys of Mary ;
Your flesh filches me from faith.
You are white as Saint Anne's child,
Fair colour and fine figure.

So sweet, under fine-spun hair,
So fair, come to the hillside.
Make our bed on a hill's breast,
Four ages under fresh birches,
The dale's green leaves its mattress,

And its fine curtains of fern,
And trees for a coverlet
To shield us from the showers.

I shall lie there like David,
Zealous prophet, for a tryst,
Solomon's father, who made
Seven psalms, for the dawnlight.
I will make, if she greets me,
Psalms of the kisses of love,
Seven the maiden's kisses,
Seven birches by the grave,
Seven vespers and masses,
Seven sermons from the thrush,
Seven leaf-covered lyrics,
Seven nightingales and boughs,
Seven strokes of ecstasy,
Seven gems, seven lyrics,
Seven songs to slim Morfudd's
Firm flesh, twenty times seven.
She will lock up no longer
The reckoning owed to love.

THE JEALOUS HUSBAND

In torment am I each day
Loving one who won't trust me.
I gave a girl love that lasts,
Iseult's face, Eiddig's fortune.
Hard for one in need, bless her,
Long grief, to hold the tall dear :
I'll not have my slim-browed girl ;
Her keeper won't allow it.
If she's in crowds, fairest girl,
A scoundrel comes to guard her.

Let Eiddig, in his vileness,
Not try to keep her his own.

Eiddig's not fond of the game,
A bitter man, not sportive,
Hates nightingale and cuckoo
And linnet more than a fox,
Nor loves, be sure, grove's shadows,
Nor singing, nor hazel nuts.
The sounds of May's small songbirds,
And green leaves, pierce him with pain.
Thrush gossip in the greenwood
And nightingale rouse his wrath.
Hateful to feeble Eiddig,
To hear harpstring and hounds.

That black Irishman Eiddig,
My mind is fixed, is my foe.
Let her part, dice-white forehead,
From her mate, nor wait six months.
I will love her forever,
I'll love none but one who's wed.
May I see the soil and rod
And rocks on the girl's husband,
Eight borrowed oxen's burden
Of turf to cover the churl.
From my estate I'd let him
Have his full measure of earth.
The girl will be seen as mine,
Iseult's man under crosses
In a hollow trench, hemp shirt,
And yellow alder coffin.

My God, if I had my choice,
He'd not live a month longer.
Planting him gives her no pain,
No pain for me to plant him.

LOVE'S ARCHITECT

I loved a pale slim maiden
For long, with never a tryst.
When I trusted, much distressed,
That she would give me gladness,
The girl I courted told me,
Refusing to hear my plea :
'I'll not love a wandering man,
No dignity, no substance.'

When I heard this quick-tongued spite,
I thought I understood her.
I made a house for loving,
No fool's work, beneath a birch,
Laid out a stately circle,
A building, plaiting of praise,
With leafy roof, tender twigs,
Like tiles at the grove's centre,
And in that pleasant dwelling
Two tenants with but one voice,
Two thrushcocks, lovely their tune,
Comely, brown, speckle-breasted,
Two poets, glowing passion,
Pure songbirds of Paradise.
Seven beautiful lyrics
To the woodbine, every day,
And the seven, lucid sound,
I'll number on the hillside.

For my darling I desired
To keep a house, this dwelling.
Should I fail to win the girl,
My own age, to the birchwood,
I'll swear, by way of payment,
Never more to build for love.

THE VIRGIN MARY

We pray to life's source, Mary,
Lady goldsmith of true health.
She is rightly named the queen,
Through her grace, heaven listens.
To hell her power reaches,
Above and across the world.
Right, fearing pain, fearing wreck
In the Channel, to name her.
Right for Mary, whom I name,
To be named a light-bearer.

Gabriel, through bright heavens,
Addressed to this holy saint
Ave, for sinful Eva ;
Mary bore that, great her grace.
Blessed was the conception,
Her Father's word, of her womb.
Good was the maid, hope's dwelling,
Her flesh bore heaven for you,
In goodness bearing her Son
And the Father who made her.
The Three, below the sun's round,
In the bright sun were dwelling.
Humbly we'll go in prayer,
As God He was born, as man.
Mary sang God lullabies
And bore Him, a pure virgin.

As the prophecy foretold
To Egypt she brought Jesus ;
The lions were light-hearted,
And the snakes, with the pure saint.
Great blessings, Mary noticed
One day when the sun was strong
A tall tree with luscious fruit
On its crest, which she craved for.

His gold love asked of Joseph
Some from the top, a bright gift.
Then angrily, in few words,
Joseph replied to Mary :
'Ask the one, fair slim maiden,
Who made you pregnant, pure saint.'
It bowed to the level earth,
That tree, by the Son's wonders ;
She had from the top her fill
Of fruit, she and her household.

None could briefly tell her Son's
Wonders worked to help Mary.
O that I, as is fitting,
Knew a hundred works to sing,
And could sing them with fine art,
And each word praising Mary.
Let us seek our lands, praying,
And 'Mary' our only word.
The Virgin does much pleading,
She will not leave men behind.
She plucks us from the briers,
And after this life, with her
Bliss for us, singing to her,
Heaven, we'll sing to Mary.

THE SALMON

Salmon, lad of the ocean,
God granted you skill and grace,
The fairest creature fashioned,
By Mary, to swim the sea.
Curig's hymn, prince of the wave,
Protects you amid seaweed,
From meshes at the tide's edge,

From hollow traps of weir-men,
From a stab and blow, the breast
Split by a poacher's trident.

Best of servants, sea trotter,
Boar of the brine, gleaming coil,
Hasten on the sea's surface,
Do not dally, swim the waves,
Take care, fish, you're unnoticed,
And go, staying out of sight,
Where dwells the girl fair-coloured
As the swallow on the wave.
No rocks, no coracle-men,
Second Llŷr, will impede you.
Once past, lord of two colours,
The rippling ford and the slope,
Bright gleaming glass, turn and look :
You'll see a splendid mansion,
A lake of water, or two,
And a terrace, and orchards.
Keep watch then, catcher of gnats,
And call the man's bed-fellow.

If you see a dark-browed girl
With a pure white complexion,
And two roses in her cheeks
A crimson red in colour,
A fine hand, as white as flour,
Wearing rings, O I'm wretched,
Slim arm like a sunlit cloud,
And breasts like the sun shining,
Two breasts as white as the snow,
More gleaming white than seagulls,
Come closer there beside her
And in my name greet that girl.
Should she come, with golden thatch,
To the brink, Luned's image,

Draw closer to my linnet,
Hurl yourself near her white breast.

I'll die of longing, woo the
Pretty girl well, salmon's mate.
Spin a story like Mordred,
From the lake near western snow.
Tell, words chosen well, take thought,
The fair one how I'm yearning.
My heart, since she's from my sight,
In my thin side is aching
For her love, pretty darling,
And what's the use ?   She's so false !
So chaste is she, this goddess,
Though she's loved, she's not possessed.
This twining vine may promise,
Never a promise is kept ;
She does not want my praises,
She trusts neither weak nor strong.

Well-bred salmon, chief witness,
Go this once to the fair girl.
Ask her if this is lawful,
Slender girl, to take my life.
Let her choose, fairest she is,
Slim Dyfr, Monmouth to Dover,
To take my life, grown feeble,
Or to leave her husband's side.

THE NUN

I have grown lean in loving
A devout and dark-eyed girl.
I'm witless, by God, if I
Woo for another's winning.

No longing for, girl I love,
Summer's fresh-springing birches ?
Will you not still the singing,
Bright star, of psalms in your house ?
The saints have your devotion,
You love your place in the choir.
God ! no more bread and water,
Throw the hateful cress away.
Mary ! stop saying your beads,
The monkish Roman credo.
Spring's no time to be a nun ;
Grove is choicer than cloister.
Your faith, fair best of women,
Is clean contrary to love :
Better the ordination
Of mantle, green gown, and ring.

Come to the outspread birches,
To the wood's and cuckoo's creed,
There no one will condemn us,
To win heaven in the grove.
Keep your mind on Ovid's book ;
An end to faith's excesses.
On the hillside we will shrive
Our souls amid the woodbines.
God's willing, blameless welcome,
And the saints, to pardon love.
Does a well-born girl do worse
Winning a soul in woodlands
Than behaving as we have
In Rome and Santiago ?

A VISIT TO FLINT

On Sunday last I came to,
I'm a man the Lord God made,

Double-walled, bastioned, bent-edged
Flint, may I see it in flames,
For a wedding, not much mead,
A feast of shifty Saxons.
I was intent on winning,
For my skill, a grand reward.

I began, I bragged boldly,
Singing an awdl to them all.
They jeered, they cut short my song,
Grief it was that I won there.
Easy for corn and barley
Dealers to spurn all my skill ;
They were laughing at my song,
Well-wrought praise, it was worthless.
Of peas John Beisir chatted,
Another about manure.

All at the board, what a bore,
Called upon William Piper.
He came, honoured by custom,
Clutching, no dignified man,
A sad bag, gut-stuffed belly,
A stick betwixt arm and breast.
He grated, strange sight, vile sound,
Swollen belly, eyes bulging,
Body twisting back and forth,
And cheeks huffing and puffing,
Coarse his ways, fingers playing
A swelled skin, shrill at the feast.
Twitching shoulders, crowd round him,
Under his cloak like flies' tails,
He snorted, as if snaffled
He ducked his head to his tit.
His movements were like a kite's,
Keen his delight in preening.

M

He blew the pipe, strange the cry,
Swelling the pouch, and yelling ;
It sang with a wasp's buzzing,
Devil's pouch, stick up its tail,
Nightmare cry, old goose butchered,
Hoarse cry, sad bitch under chest,
Shrill belly screeching one tune,
Gristle mouth wheezing music,
A crane's monotonous cry,
Goose honking under apron.
In the hollow bag were sounds
Like a thousand cats' tendons,
Unwanted goat with one note,
Dirty, diseased, and pregnant.

When it ended, mad girl's song,
This squeal, it would quell passion,
William Beanbroth paid the fees,
Not a lordly hand's largesse,
Some pennies, where they offered,
And small halfpennies from some ;
And me turned angrily from
The foolish feast, hands empty.

I renounce with solemn vow
Cramped Flint and all its offspring :
Its furnace shall be like hell,
Saxon people and piper.
I pray only for their deaths,
I curse them and their children.
If I go again, ever,
May I not come back alive.

LENT

The day of Eiddig's delight
Came yesterday, I'm wretched,
A day to burden a bard
Like the world's end, Shrove Tuesday,
Start of the way to heaven,
God guiding all burdened men.
For forty days there's pardon
For praying with piety.

My Lord, each day this season
Is doled out just like a year.
Long for me, I'm in exile,
Three days of the life I lead.
The anchorite's Roman creed
Is mine, like a lean scribbler ;
True am I to their credo,
True is the girl, she'll show love
By setting us, like Fridays,
Mortifying acts for Lent.
Farewell, my slim-waisted girl,
All's chaste till Easter Monday.
Not one sight, not one night will
I go to meet her till then.
I'll ask not a kiss, sweetheart,
Nothing of my lovely dear.

When Easter's in the greenwood,
She'll come each day to the tryst ;
The price she'll pay is wearing
No damask till Easter-time.
Then at last our day will come
Brimming with exultation,
May and summer, where she is,
Cuckoos like Gwgon's daughter,

Each birch-grove wearing fine hair,
Green-gowned, weighed down with tresses,
Along the street of thorn-stems
Linen shops like London's Cheap,
Dewdrops and shoots in gardens,
Wine berries, ridges of wheat,
Clear sky and blue-capped ocean,
A close screen in the green grove,
A lovely spot, a clearing,
A slim fair limb of a girl,
An end of all our penance,
And grief ebbs, and the world turns.
Our curse from this time forward
On the cold and windy Spring.

Siôn Cent

THE BARDS

False words, false is the yardstick,
Welshmen flee, a foolish path.
Why the old man's sweet language ?
To prove how a bard performs.
Two sorts of fluent muses
The world has, in bright array :
Christ's muse, no mournful topic,
On a true course, honest muse,
This was theirs, full of blessings,
Prophets and masters of praise,
Holy angels in Hebron
Fashioning their faultless verse ;
The other, foolish singing
That trusts in a filthy lie,
This was theirs, reckless men,
The high bards of Wales' burden.

If he praises a soldier,
Singing for a silly robe,
The artless song's a satire,
He sings a cywydd of lies,
Saying there's noble vintage
And mead where there's merely whey,
Proclaiming, high table's words,
Of fiercely won French castles.
A Roland, a bold Arthur,
He's a lion in the fray.
Their feuds, a shame none know them,
Their evil ways and their aims.
A poor man's praised, lying song,
More than any, bleak region,
More than an earl, gold paving,

And more than an emperor.
The foolish man's fond of praise,
Trusts it like oaths on relics.
O God, which fool's the greatest,
The man or the best of bards ?

If he sings to a maiden
Or a wife, by the true Cross,
No Mary in three countries
Nor the sun was bright as she.

He sings, unskilled, that he's a
Lord or a prince of gold praise :
He's a boor, belly and claw,
Patched and scabby and crumpled.
No loudly crying image
Or cur could be worse than he.

A good spirit, sober sire,
God-fostered, speaks no falsehood,
No smooth-tongued fraud, no folly,
No false song, fabulous lie.
There are dicta in ten shires
Of truth's guard, Thomas Lombard :
Each lie, in detail, each day,
However small, is sinful.
So testifies the steady
Sense of Alysanna's book,
Or Durgry's book, much sought-for,
Precious title, only look :
These bards and their bold falsehoods
For slander of furious folk,
Swords in mind, proper welcome,
Treated, they all were, as Jews.
If a Welshman's, I submit,
Bard, or a humble minstrel,
If he knows how to answer,
Let his lips make answer now.

THE PURSE

My velvet purse, my parson,
My golden coffer, my cure,
My much-praised guard, my prophet,
My friend speaking but one tongue,
No finer guard, free-giving,
Nest of gold, beneath the sky,
None pays off strangers better :
Many thanks, my purse, for this.

I owned stallions, was honoured,
Jewels, weapons, precious stuff,
Brilliant gems, and heavy rings,
Chains, nine bundles of brooches ;
Dressed beyond, splendid fellow,
My land and station in life ;
Many my men in Emlyn :
Many thanks, my purse, for this.

I've studied Solomon's book,
The seven arts and speaking ;
I've studied heavenly things,
Calm lamp of churchly wisdom ;
I've studied to use, men's mead,
With bold stroke, battle's conquest,
Awdl and cywydd and englyn :
Many thanks, my purse, for this.

Claiming a kinship with me
Plenty of well-off people,
Nine times more, blows to my joy,
Than all my kin, came calling ;
I have, surely, eight kinds of kin,
A life full of sworn brothers ;
All country tramps, all paupers,
All minstrels, all sick of sea,

All beaten men come begging :
Many thanks, my purse, for this.

Fine is wealth, says famed Gwenddydd,
Fine for us is every day,
The world's stock of food, of drink,
All things in finest fashion ;
I'm welcomed, a friendly name,
Sweet word, abroad, like Menw ;
I'm honoured in each market,
Throned at each feast in my land ;
With deep respect I'm treated :
Many thanks, my purse, for this.

If a theft is traced surely
To me, and I'm brought to court,
If trial or judgment comes,
I know I'll win acquittal ;
Forty will swear, quite meekly,
Lies, on three Sundays, for me ;
Friendly are the officials,
All of them, in trying me ;
My gem of gold, my herald :
Many thanks, my purse, for this.

I've had much love from women,
Consent I'd gain with a gift,
Love's heralds in Is Conwy,
A million, had I so willed ;
No need to leave the tavern
All my life, if I think fit,
Such grabbing at the elbows
For me, bringing me to mead ;
I'm honoured, act of homage :
Many thanks, my purse, for this.

For gold I'll have, I take pains,
The whole world, full of pleasure ;

I'll have all Wales, none missing,
Houses and castles and land ;
I'll have the love of heaven,
God for my flesh, solemn thought,
Life for my name, my soul saved,
And win Papal indulgence,
And all the foe's war finished :
Many thanks, my purse, for this.

REPENTANCE

It is in my mind to pray
To God and to His Mother.
High time for me, Saul's status,
To cease worldly wantonness.

I've borne, without amending,
A wicked burden of sins :
Pride in the midst of many,
Filthy work, an evil life,
And with pride my habit's been
False praise and defamation ;
Envy has permeated,
Perversion of faith, my flesh ;
And wrath, where it might enter,
Unhappy load, was no less ;
Sloth till the grave, I was rash,
The life I led was lazy ;
God, weed a man ! greed was worse,
In covetousness drowning ;
Gluttony, adultery,
These two were adversaries.

Three enemies come to man
To offer means for mischief,

The filthy world, the devil,
The flesh, reaping Judas' crop.
Woe's the man, I know his fault,
Wanton, who cannot govern
His life till he's in the grave,
Well prepared for his finish,
Chastizing reckless evil
And the body's subtle ways.

My infection I confess,
Of God I beg forgiveness.
I reveal every secret,
I attempt to tell in full,
Rash pride, fearless and endless,
How I lived when I was young :
Straying in fern and birches
And green woods above the glen,
Hearing and speaking wrongly
Of love's doings, magic ring,
Touching wrongly, clear concord,
Seeking good, hating its source,
The arrogance and envy,
Wicked glances at a girl,
Praise of, unblest, unbridled,
Beauty, breaking marriage vows.

Wantonness brings on a man
Its revenge if long followed,
Unless he makes atonement
To God before the day comes.
Let none wait for, foul marshes,
Repentance after his death.
I weep, I call on Heaven
And Mary before I die,
For a bright, blissful dwelling
For my soul in need.   Amen.

THE VANITY OF THE WORLD

Mortal flesh is full of grief,
The world, cold thing, 's a sermon.

Today a gay man of gold
Has brooches, rings, and jewels,
Heaps of scarlet and camlet,
And fine silk, if it's in vogue,
Splendid drinking-horns of gold,
Wine and kestrels and falcons.
Mounted on Gascon stallions
He rides before, and all bow.
To ask for a good farmhold
On his lands is an offence ;
He gets a weak man under
His thumb, and seizes his place,
Takes his farm from one who's blind,
And takes another's acres,
Takes the grain under ashtrees,
Takes an innocent man's hay,
Collects two hundred cattle,
Gets the goods, and jails the man.

Futile the frantic plotting
Of weak clay, dead in a day.
From bare earth he came, dark cold,
Coldly he goes in ashes.
Two cows he'd not surrender
Yesterday, for two from God !
Today in earth he's worthless,
Of all his goods he has none.
Pain fills him, when he goes there,
Covered with gravel and grit ;
His bed will be much too base,
His forehead next the roof-beam ;
His tight-belted robe the shroud,

His cradle earth and gravel ;
The porter above his head
Earth black as a nightmare ;
His proud flesh in an oak-chest,
His nose a pale sorry grey ;
His coat of mail black with grime,
Its fringes all have rusted ;
His robe wood, grief's constriction,
His shirt without sleeves or shape ;
His sure road into this earth,
His arms across his bosom ;
His walks vacant, gone the wine,
His cook deserts his kitchen ;
His hounds, in the empty hall,
His steeds, in doubt about him ;
His wife, from the drinking hall,
Quite rightly, weds another ;
His stately whitewashed mansion
A small coffin the world sp ɩs ;
The wealth of the wo   ɩeaves him
Down below with ɪpty hands.

When in his honoured coffin
He's speeded from court to church,
No pretty girl will follow,
No healthy man, past the grave.
No slender wanton will slide
Her hand beneath that blanket.
No grief will long continue
Nor lie a month on his grave.
When for an hour he's lain there,
This man with long yellow hair,
Should he notice, dark the house,
A toad will tend his bedside.
Under the neck of the stone
More fat worms than fair branches.
Around him in earth's sad house

More coffins than great stallions.
The choir priests detest dealing
With the three executors :
Three hundred pounds in payment
Received for their services ;
His kin above will be proud
If they complete three masses.
There the spirit will possess
No mansion, rank, or favour,
No ornament, no idols,
Only what it did for God.

Where are the towers ? the town ?
The many courts ? the singers ?
The gabled houses ? the land ?
The high places for merit ?
Where's the morsel ? the new dish
The roast ? the cook who serves i .
Where's the wine ? the birds ? th boughs
Carried throughout the country ?
The wine-cellar ? the kitchen
Under the hill ? Where's the m d ?
The trip to England ? the gear
The splendid bards ? the dais ?
Where are the huge gentle hounds ?
The flock of swans ? the stallions ?
The full wardrobe ? the treasure ?
Possessions on land and sea,
The great hall newly enclosed,
The palaces, the mansions ?
There remains no small holding,
Only seven feet, man's end.

The flesh, once wrapped in purple,
Lies in a chest next the choir,
And there the soul does not know,
Dim-witted, where it's going.

For the wrongs and heresies
Committed in his lifetime,
That dark day, as I'm a man,
Is too late for repentance.
There not one of his hundred
He'll reward, that sleep's too long ;
Not one fellow will follow,
He'll not conquer, nor bear arms,
Nor love girls, nor be greeted,
Nor pace through council and court ;
He'll have no mead for a spree,
Nor leave the grave to revel.
I'd not give a head of leek
For his corpse in the coffin.

The soul, shuttled shamefully,
Between ice and fire, freezes,
Where he's compelled, no shelter,
To a close compact with cold.
What help in a hall of ice ?
Beware, the pit is frightful.
Pools and infernal ovens,
Cauldrons, dragons, devils' shapes ;
See each beast, Christ is mighty,
Horned and tusked and glowering ;
The hand of every devil
Holds a crooked cooking fork ;
And a smoky blackness like
Flood-tide's treacherous onslaught.
May Christ, that place is dreadful,
Preserve men from going there !

Learn that there's a worldly state
Leads many to the devil.
Holy Saint Benedict says
God gives only one heaven.
Just one may, eloquent words,

Be won, though helped by Mary.
Let no man in the pleasure
Of lust find his heaven here,
Lest he lose, say the masters,
Eternal heaven through sin :
Day without night is displayed,
Health without drawn-out illness,
The gaily coloured face of
Heaven's land, better than wealth.
This world fails, a nest of twigs,
But heaven lasts for ever,
Without end, all men as one,
Amen, O Son of Mary !

Llywelyn ap y Moel

THE WOOD OF THE GREY CRAG

By God, Wood, you are lovely,
Grey hill, prey-concealing Crag.
Circle of leaves, Irish snare,
God's blessing on your branches.
Closely ranked is your array,
A place for sport, a fortress.

Cosy house, close of bracken,
Strange is the summer if one
Can do, sure servant of love,
Without you, as I see it,
The tapestry of your twigs,
Your hills, your leafy towers.
You're my prince, my paradise,
My safe honour, my partner,
My patron saint, sure warrant,
My haven, my manor hall.

Flawless growth, how good it's been
To have you as my safeguard,
A sweet close, a snug cover,
A securely plaited hedge,
A level place beneath me,
Dear land of green, a lord's gem,
Cluster of delightful leaves,
Tent of darkness above me.
Mine is a bed in safety,
Your twigs above are not like
A churl's hut, a turf rooftop,
Fine after dining on oats.

Better far than bard's roaming
For a man who's after good,

To take a Saxon, strip him
Beneath your twigs, pleasant spot,
And broadcast rage and riot,
And cut leaves, teacher of lore,
And hear from a fair castle,
Pure-voiced song, the nightingale.
Many times, I trust to you,
I've been trailed round a hilltop.
Snowy paths, trackless region,
Where by night no Northmen pass,
Broad circle about our perch,
To Owain's men you're London.

The state of England decays,
God let your soldiers triumph !
All blessings upon my side,
Full reward, men of Owain !

THE BATTLE OF WAUN GASEG

We began quite well today,
Full warband, on a hilltop,
Mighty, men of flawless gold,
With splendid proud intentions,
Set on gaining, bright emblem,
For Owain the greatest fame.
We met, no mind to appeal,
Before we left for battle,
Declared our aim of sharing
The spoils if the foe were slain,
And each one gave his firmest
Oath, before seeing their men,
Not to flee, they would earn fame,
The field before the onslaught.

N

And so, after our singing
A plea to bountiful God,
Look there ! we saw upon us,
Loose in our midst, sorry fate,
All along a fern-clad slope
More than a hundred horses,
And with them, case for appeal,
The shrill and blaring clamour
Of a gilt bugler's harsh tune,
A fierce French badger-keeper,
Ape-faced, sounding the tabor,
A horn louder than a gun.
Worthless warband, passage barred,
We, after all our speeches,
Stayed on the moor in battle
For no longer than an hour.
Sword untried, leap of terror,
And coat of mail when we fled.

That warband took its wrath out
In hunting close after us.
Hot they were to pursue us,
They chased us across nine brooks,
Prize of the men of Caer Wysg,
Chasing goats, in gay clothing.
For pride a sad adventure :
It pained us to see, I swear,
On Waun Gaseg, white burden,
Our men's spears upon the grass.

And I won, vile distinction,
A front place fleeing the fray,
Running in quite a hurry
To a gorge, great host behind,
All pointing at me fleeing
When they recognized me there.

Slow on a sloping mountain's
A man in white, hapless task.

Because of this, painless summons,
They may return when they choose :
I'm damned if they shall see me
White-clad in the glen of Waun !

Lewis Glyn Cothi

THE SWORD

The lion with golden mane
Who lives down in Croes Oswallt,
Mighty Dafydd ap Gutun,
May he never grow white hair.
He's Arthur, bestowing wine,
And Uthr of Ieuan Get'in.
He is of Cuhelyn's clan.
He's lord of the sea border,
The Ifor Hael of Maelor,
Efrog of Cyfeiliog's length.
Let him lead, beneath the crown,
Powys, grandson of Dafydd.

His grandsires held two strong lands,
They're Mechain and long Mochnant :
One grandson holds against all
Arundel's land united.
To Dover, like Dafydd's herds,
His fame, Job's fortune, reaches.
To the land he's a great mart,
To Oswallt town a treasure,
Himself almost more lavish
Than twelve with his wealth to them.
God's begrudged by a miser :
From him, it takes but a sign.
This request I make Dafydd,
It's given before I ask,
Not for gold, and not for land,
A sword, one of his weapons.

It has, for proper gripping,
A short hilt round as a cask ;

There's a white-corniced cover,
And a clamp like a round ring.
There's a belt, forked and crooked,
A wooden sheath and bent cross.
By the cross, it's so fashioned,
It is broader than a hand.
It has a point that's as thin
As a wing's tip, a needle,
A thorn like a fine-honed dart,
Keen steel, two feet three inches,
Blest cross against boorish boys,
Protecting cross, stripped naked.
Blue blade, when it is displayed,
Sheet of glass like a razor,
A light it is, a long crutch,
And like true gold it glitters,
Killer, like a Jew's dagger,
And keen as a lion's tooth.

This I request of Dafydd,
If this request he will grant,
I will shave, by Saint Non's hand,
All of the lads of Chester.
On every churl I'll whet it,
Rib of steel, if I come there.
Not one leaves, till Saint Dwyn's Feast,
The hot town head unbroken.
I'll carve, if I come near them,
Twenty thousand naked curs.
That day, after drinking wine,
I'll wield the blade of Cyffin,
I'll deal with my hands a hurt
To that two-faced town yonder.

From the towns of Rhos at dawn,
By nightfall to dark Chester :

Let me kill, if my day arrives,
With Dafydd's sword two thousand !

THE COVERLET

Gold Angharad, silver hand,
Gave wine once to one feeble :
I wish for such lavish gifts,
Elin, Môn's merry daughter.

She's the lily on the lawn,
Sun of courteous Llywelyn,
The planet of Prysaddfed,
She is Hwlcyn's glowing moon,
The Non of ancient Ynyr,
Non of Nannau's line and men,
Crest of Merioneth's Meirig,
Leaves of Cynddelw of Môn.
Saint Catherine of the wine,
Elin, Llywelyn's daughter,
And like a balm from Elin
One is served five sorts of wine.
Her hand's open to many,
Elin's feast, Elen of hosts.
Derfel's blessing to Elin,
Noble crest of Gwynedd's wine.
She's praised, Llywydiarth's lady,
From her land to Aber Arth :
Too much, by Saint Garmon's Church,
In Môn my lack of manners.

Go, complaint, to Gwynedd's sun,
I complain of the mongrels,
So crafty they were, so cold,
Mobs in the town of Chester.

It's they who plundered my house
Of my bed and fine bedspread,
And they have left me barer
Than salmon swimming a stream.

Elin will give me once more,
Free-handed, a pied cover,
A tapestry of vineleaves,
Small torch as broad as the trees.
Coverlet of nine colours,
Nine birds there are on its cloth,
Nine stags upon the hillsides,
With nine hinds of the same kind,
And twelve leaves of varied blue,
Lovely dark and blue shading
A hundred of green and white,
A thousand of red and yellow,
Small pictures, girl's handiwork,
Oaks, and birds in the clearing,
Sky that hides a man's forehead,
The cloth's a dapple-green sky.
The gift will stay till summer.
No cold night, no frost for me.
Elin spreads on my bare bed
Every night a green banner.

Mahallt, Hywel Selau's child,
Because of words that praised her,
Gave a coverlet in need,
For song, a bed to Gwilym.
My lady, mistress of Môn,
Will give this time another.
I come, Cynfrig ap Dafydd,
I go there, to daylight's hue.
Easy for me to ask for
Her gold and gifts, Ithael's child,
And a feast from Cynfrig's hand,

Wealth from the hands of Elin.
A coverlet on my bed,
Grace to the hands that grant it,
And to Cynfrig and Elin
Three lifetimes bestowing wine !

LAMENT FOR SIÔN Y GLYN

One boy, Saint Dwyn, my bauble :
His father rues he was born !
Sorrow was bred of fondness,
Lasting pain, lacking a son.
My two sides, dead is my die,
For Siôn y Glyn are aching.
I moan everlastingly
For a baron of boyhood.

A sweet apple and a bird
The boy loved, and white pebbles,
A bow of a thorntree twig,
And swords, wooden and brittle ;
Scared of pipes, scared of scarecrows,
Begging mother for a ball,
Singing to all his chanting,
Singing 'Oo-o' for a nut.
He would play sweet, and flatter,
And then turn sulky with me,
Make peace for a wooden chip
Or the dice he was fond of.

Ah that Siôn, pure and gentle,
Cannot be a Lazarus !
Beuno once brought back to life
Seven who'd gone to heaven ;
My heart's sorrow, it's doubled,
That Siôn's soul is not the eighth.

Mary, I groan, he lies there,
And my sides ache by his grave.
The death of Siôn stands by me
Stabbing me twice in the chest.
My boy, my twirling taper,
My bosom, my heart, my song,
My prime concern till my death,
My clever bard, my daydream,
My toy he was, my candle,
My fair soul, my one deceit,
My chick learning my singing,
My Iseult's chaplet, my kiss,
My strength, in grief he's left me,
My lark, my weaver of spells,
My bow, my arrow, my love,
My beggar, O my boyhood.
Siôn is sending his father
A sword of longing and love.

Farewell the smile on my mouth,
Farewell to my lips' laughter,
Farewell sweet consolation,
Farewell the begging for nuts,
Farewell, far-off the ballgame,
Farewell to the high-pitched song,
Farewell, while I stay earthbound,
My gay darling, Siôn my son.

Dafydd Nanmor

THE PEACOCK

Brilliant peacock, gown gleaming,
Far-seen shimmer glossy gown,
Greet, best of loves and gracious,
Green-winged you are Gwen o'r Ddôl.
Cross over the fords yonder
To Eiddig's, no good to him.
Shining cowl, see how things stand,
Between those two breed hatred.

May's lovely mantle is yours,
The plumes of birds and flowers.
Most closely, an enchanter,
You resemble barley ears.
Like a roof and hall of leaves
Are you, a bird's fair bower.
In your hoop, small comely roof,
Thousands of golden wafers.
The same texture, new curtain,
Has your hue as leaves of yew.
A golden angel's image,
You are wearing golden wings.
Speckled you are, like sound cloth,
A friar's cloth embroidered.
Mild bird, red-gold's your colour,
Fair twigs filled with marigolds.
The semblance, no ill omen,
Of a multitude of moons.
Wings of gold like a bishop,
A noble's no better hue,
Speckled and outstretched pinions,
Gold buttons on their tips.
Fair, peacock, above the glade,

The same hue as a rainbow.
A fair sight, like coils are you,
Green dragon of church windows.

Go to the spot, passion's choice,
And hurry, azure adder,
And come there like a fowler,
Fetch Gwen from her husband's home !

LAMENT FOR GWEN

To trust in the world brings grief,
Life is a brief illusion.
I loved a slender young girl,
And she died, the fair maiden.
Black fate (where's one so blameless ?)
To place that face under earth.
If her cheeks have been covered,
Less warmth in many a cheek.
If died six times her number,
None like her in that large grave.
O God, if she's been buried,
Why could I not be her shroud ?
Have I life, and her, dumbstruck,
Shovel under while I live ?

Widowed of her on hillsides
Are cuckoo, birches, and woods,
Song of thrush, if she's under
The church, and brown nightingale.
If she's dead in Is Conwy,
No more should May put forth leaves.
Withered, birches and branches,
And they will bear no leaves now.
If the maiden died in May,
O why is she dead, Mary ?

Why not for me, O wretched,
Both of us dead the same day ?
I'd not wish my life longer
When she has no fuller life.
O to lie for a single
Hour with the girl in her grave !
Wretched am I without her,
A horned ox above my Gwen.
They are dead, to my thinking,
The fair sun, the selflessness.
I'm lost unless she rises,
From the dead, sweetheart, to life ;
No more, a pound I'll wager,
One like the sun's seen on roads.
There was not, when she was well,
Under dark brows one fairer.

Lazarus, once, did Jesus
Raise from the grave, he was dead :
Let God act, bright slender girl,
And raise for me a maiden.
Dark am I as a leaf on
A yew-twig, if Gwen has died.
Let her be the eighth pure soul,
Slim girl, brought back by Beuno !

NOBILITY

Rhys, rose blossom of summer,
Rhys' grandson, no lowly strain,
Nobleness was your groundwork,
All Deheubarth's offering.
You're our heritage and home,
Right foot of Tywyn's region.

You grow as the ashtrees grow
From multitudes of chieftains.
Grain will grow, like summer wheat,
No crest where roots are lacking :
Who grows from noble breeding
Grows from his roots to his crest.
Good is summer, stag roaming,
For the wheat and for the vines :
Good for one of his sires' stock,
His fashioning by chieftains.
There's no place that is not pure
In the book of John's Gospel :
Fewer the stains, where it was,
Found in your book of lineage.
The stag's antlers grow larger,
It's good blood that breeds a king :
The nobles, as an heir's nursed,
Foster the noble virtues.

Two streams in the valley
Cause high water in the lake :
To you went your father's state,
Nobleness makes you chieftain.
Never has the grain perished
In the wellspring of July :
No man, no peasants' rising,
Has ever dishonoured you.
On a bright day there's no snow,
Sun glowing on the hillside :
No man leans but from fondness
Above you, the land's right arm.
Well does one swim a river
If his hair's kept clear of waves :
You went where they did not come,
You're on shore, through the currents.
Slow one goes up a hillside,
With a load, against the grade :

Harder, when you were younger,
To bear your mouth's hostile word.

The salmon seeks fresh water,
The same wave his father took :
Your father's state is higher
Than the mountains of the Alps.
Of deer who race on a slope
The strongest wins the hilltop :
Take the slope, like a roebuck,
To the breach Maredudd left.
A huntsman pursues the trail,
To the wind the hawk rises,
The stag's eager for summer,
The lion for lofty paths :
Come, the tree's crest and blossom !
Come, eagle, to the oak's crest !
On the crest of nobleness
Are you, Rhys, like sea on shore.

To you has come a high rank,
Will come your father's fortune.
To you, Rhys, your chin burdened,
May Moses' life's measure come !

Rhys Goch Eryri

THE FOX

Fox, white of tail, most wicked,
Fine slim dog, you crave fresh meat ;
You crave a green-grove banquet
Near a meadow, hound of lambs.
Hear this song, you'll dine on duck,
And on goose, it should suit you.
A fat bird you'll have, you're sly,
You're a most clever trickster,
Bold on a slope, white belly,
And a plucky pilferer.

Where are your words of wisdom ?
Give me them, fox, about this :
I love tender-hearted Gwen
Of the Dale, cheeks like Helen's,
And another, hard on me,
Fool from Eryri loves her.
Dafydd, an upright poet,
Nanmor is his famous name.
My plaint to you is pointed
At his peacock, dainty-gowned,
Which, like a white-fringed greenwood,
Is love's herald to Gwen's home,
And that moon, Eigr of many,
He tries to take with a trick.
If he wins her, white seagull,
With many-hued magic cloak,
He'll bear Gwen from her husband
To this lad, beneath his cape.

If the old goose you long for,
Daring wild dog, you'll have three,

Go to the Dale, a good hen
And a lambkin you'll win there.
And walk amidst the bracken
Round the Dale, guard a fine girl,
And stay clear of loud noises,
Eiddig's gun, his dogs and men.
The peacock spied, fine sentry,
Then at him, my shepherd fox !
Bold thief, try to herd him home,
Gwen of the Dale's enchanter.
To whatever spot, furclad
Small dog of thickets, he goes,
Watch the place where he's dwelling,
Meat for a fee, dog, you'll have,
And revenge upon his jaws
His flight to hold Gwen spellbound.
I beg you, forestall his leap,
Rip the gold mantle's fringes,
Slay Llawdden's twin, love's herald,
Take his fine gown and his head.

As for Gwen, her brow's slender,
It's between me and that bard.
With song, if he is noble,
For that gown we'll have a joust.

THE VISION OF SAINT BEUNO

Fine the wisdom, mournful men,
The gentle words of sages :
Magnificence, thousands' praise,
Of the earthly world's regions,
Is vanity, easy course,
And evil in God's presence.
Is there one, by Christ's Father,
Will follow a hero's lead ?

One may see, majestic feast,
What Hugh the Strong accomplished.
For greater emperors' praise
He chose for Charles a banquet.
Not a man, far as day stretched,
On earth, of God's baptizing,
Hosts of Constantinople,
Or noble would not be there.
Now there is mighty boasting,
Fine contention, at the feast.
The feast of Hugh and the kings
And the vast legion vanished,
It went to earth from anger
In ashes, like a lost thing.

A great man's feast, majestic,
I know, topping gold and gems.
No likeness, that borrowed food,
Here to Hugh Ploughman's banquet,
The angelic feast, praise be,
And ritual of triumph
Of God's grace, His state is best,
Sweet prize, to Abbot Beuno.
The seventh day, unstinting,
Before Easter, known by all,
When Beuno, marble tomb's lord,
Was, this ascetic noble,
Wise lord, away from his church,
This leader, on his sickbed,
His shirt of mail, most joyful,
Golden binding, on his breast,
With fair cross, gold-clad banquet,
And small cross (who's known more grace?)
And clear lamp, gleaming crozier,
Bright flame-colour, ripened fruit,
True pomp's course, ceaseless bounty,
God's image in his fair hands,

o

Beuno, there was priceless pomp,
Saw, a sunbeam's strong journey,
Gleaming gates, where bounty's found,
And the whole city open,
Lofty throne, gold assembly,
The place of the Trinity.
He saw, rarer than riches,
The holy tower, the land.
He saw, himself, that same hour,
A greater good, God's martyrs.
He saw four, fine musician,
Archangels of purest gold,
With crowns, the country's honours,
On the face of the gold sky,
Performing each pure office
For the Man who nourished them.
He saw the twelve splendid lamps,
Men well placed in God's circle,
Heaven's treasure richly clad,
Fair, fair, beside the Father.
He saw high upon May's breast
David and faultless Deiniol,
Song of grace, a hundred-fold,
Brightly gleaming in glory.
He saw all who were with them,
And he heard, a splendid note,
True omen, bright heaven's lord,
Glorious God invite him,
Calling unasked, there honoured,
To Beuno to come on high.

A blessed man, throne's burden,
Was Beuno the innocent,
Fine prize when he was chosen,
Fine hero, by God's mouth,
For the feast, lasting goodness,
Golden virtue without end.

Think not, numberless notion,
Unworthy man's worldly gifts,
This feast, with its unceasing
Sharing, like Hugh's ancient feast.
Peter, as Pope, dear brave lord,
And Paul in the bright heavens
Beuno, that worthy saint, saw,
Precious praise, having manna.
He saw, a marvellous tale,
The blessings of all virgins,
Fair belief, like bright hailstones,
And Mary, sun in their midst.
He saw Paradise' bright land,
Its white walls, its fair sanctum,
And the four rivers, fair waves,
Running rapidly through it,
Wine and milk, fair lion's mouth,
Praise of faith, oil and honey.
This God, from His graciousness,
Fine courtesy, gave Beuno,
For water, no coward's prize,
A world of case, and barley,
Which Beuno, the hero, took
For God, almighty Father,
Heavy the pain of penance,
Way of pain, while in the world.

The day there passed, lightly bound,
The living soul from Beuno,
God commanded, splendid deed,
In language holy Beuno
To leave the gold flesh at once
Surrounding there his spirit,
Golden praise, and come fairly,
Best of needs, with all his speed,
To possess, unfading light,
The angels' land and banquet,

Fair and boundless residence,
Wise leader, everlasting,
With the Father on the throne,
Son, Holy Ghost, and Mary.
Beneath the throne's banner dwells
Blessed innocent Beuno,
Open honour, unhindered,
Amen, is that not his place ?

Llywelyn ap Gutun

THE DROWNING OF GUTO'R GLYN

All over Wales they're grieving,
Town and field, for Guto'r Glyn,
Drowned on a tideless seastrand,
In heaven : he could not swim.
Wasted for me that action
Had I no lament in mind.
Never will such, marble slabs,
Big hands steer through the ocean.
The drowning of his body
Will better the seashore's verse.
Woe's me, for his triple dip,
His purse not in my clutches !
I saw him spin like a wheel
Off Malltraeth, nose for pivot.
Woe's me, my worst misfortune,
Gone the man's cloak and his cap !

Take, all of you, two fierce cheeks,
A fool to mock for Christmas.
In the sea, I must say it,
There's a bear-face, one I know ;
Mackerels in his ribcage,
More than a school, near the mud ;
There's a great lump of a fish,
A seal, in my friend's bosom ;
Men find, in the false river,
Herrings coming from his boots.
The cradle of the cywydd
Is now a hollow for eels.

My warrior went by water,
And his song went with the wind.

203

See there, a mortar in size,
A bard's form filled with dogfish.
The wave come from the water
Would not leave the fords he strolled
But on the one side held him
Gripped fast, and gave him a shove.
It was strong, he's in motion,
The seashells stick in his hand ;
On his horse he is driven
To and fro, a wicked shame.

There are jealous men joyful
To bury the cywydd's hawk.
Who'll be the old bards' captain ?
The great oak over the bards ?
Where's the kite's executor ?
Who'll sing now ? a sea-spirit ?
Who will prevent him, hag-cheeked,
Pinning the chair on his robes ?
Who but the ghost of Gwido
Will halt him and hew him down ?

One greater than the wizard,
A phantom, walks in his steps.
Not one sail is setting course,
It's not the one-time Guto,
But is, calf's feet and figure,
A gown around Gwido's ghost.
A spectre, like a bullock,
Has stalked through the smoke of Môn.
Ferocious face, he's driven
A swarm of priests scurrying.
Let them in their turn drive him
To God or the devil's hand.

Guto'r Glyn

THE DRUNKEN DREAM OF LLYWELYN

A sad wail like the waters
Off Malltraeth, much worse than saints :
A minstrel's meditating
My lament, dead in the deep.
Wise Llywelyn ap Gutun,
Does he foam less than that flood ?

Harpist, and poetry's prize,
He's dunking bards on benches.
True lyrist and ladies' man,
Splendid lad, who is like him ?
His lip lively and flawless,
His nails even livelier.
Woe's me, he's wise and witty
Until his head's full of wine.
Drinking makes his clever tongue
Turn ever on the water.

It's he who saw my image
Brine-soaked off Môn in his sleep.
This fellow was in Llwydiarth :
And I was drowned ? Was he drunk ?
Cynfrig's wine, a potent gift,
And Huw's wine made him helpless.
To Huw Lewis' court and land
Came high tide for a harpist,
And he dreamed, to drown minstrels,
That the flood rose to the roof.
Llywelyn's sons did battle,
Filling him full of their drink.
He roared, this lying Welshman,
Me here, fire there, counting waves.

He's swearing, that's where I strand,
That I'm a wraith in Malltraeth,
That in me, grim existence,
Fish are coming to the shore,
A seal is in my bosom,
Or my spirit's in the creel.
He paid me heed, my saviour,
In the sea he made my grave.
He wants me at rest in ocean :
He craves my cloak and my sword.
In cosy clay he'd plant me,
For my gold, above the ford.
He'd hang me, without a peep,
In Rhosyr for my clothing.
A dream that proved no portent
Had this lad upon Môn's land.
My drowning he imagined :
Despite the drowning, I lived.

The dream I'd see Thursday night,
Saint Non's Day, would have substance :
There goes his wealth at Melwern
Washed to the heart of The Bog,
And him also, in his hall,
Awash, the river kills him,
The Efyrnwy over him,
And, at its mouth, the ocean.
I think, when he's extinguished,
To fling a lament in too.

Let's both float, he was my friend,
(Heaven for the dead !) the seas :
If to hell we are sentenced,
Let him gain the shore he left ;
If heaven, the swim's simpler,
Then my soul will turn to Môn.

WILIAM HERBART

Three warbands went into Wales,
They thrust their way through Gwynedd,
Yr Pil's forces, Lord Wiliam's,
The Viscount's, that was their goal.
Three ways, ancient Offa's Dyke,
Wiliam journeys, Sarn Elen.
Lord Herbart, with your wagons
And your warband, God's your guide :
Before, all forces found rain ;
Now, when you come, fair weather.
I foresaw you'd have Gwynedd,
Take Môn for the man who rules.

The English, they'd give their eyes,
Were Harlech sieged, to have it.
Thick-trunked tale of enmity,
Sharp-tipped for foolish people :
Sharp-tipped tale, your twist and turn,
Thick-trunked ruler of Pembroke.
What better fort against siege,
Now Pembroke's wall is broken ?
You hurled, shook till it tumbled,
Carreg Cennen to the glen.
The trenches above Harlech
Held no better than a pen.
No house stays you, no tower,
No white fort, no conqueror.

Three bands from your three lands went
Through Gwynedd, claps of thunder,
Three parties, their captains proud,
Three bands, nine thousand yeomen,
Your brothers, soldiers who rule,
Your land, the South and Gwynedd.
All your men, they are heroes,

They are dragons through the woods.
Your mounts, where sheep would not go,
Climbed the belly of Snowdon.
On crags you leave your traces,
You turn Snowdonia to tilth.
Your men split in three sections
Through moorland and wilderness.
If you kindled a fire then
With total war and slaughter,
It was insurrection's scourge,
Ripping and whipping Gwynedd.

If the land's been, brave Herbart,
Faithless, so once was Saint Paul :
Wrath's to blame for what has been ;
When that ends, they'll be christened.
And you, on your part, be not
Savage, loosing fire on men.
Kill not the hawks who feast us
In Gwynedd like Peter's bees.
Put no tax on that region
It's powerless to collect.
Flay not till Gwynedd's fallow,
Nor surrender Môn to wrath.
Let the feeble complain of,
Henceforth, neither fraud nor theft.

Keep Horsa's offspring from Flint,
Rowena's race from Gwynedd.
No posts for Saxons, my lord,
No pardon for a burgess.
Judge rightly, king of our tongue,
Cast in the fire their honours.
Take men of Wales, this moment,
Lord from Barnstable to Môn.
Take Morgannwg and Gwynedd,
Make one land, Conwy to Nedd.

Should England's dukes be angered,
Wales will be there in your need !

LAMENT FOR LLYWELYN AP Y MOEL

There is in Ystrad Marchell
A coffin amidst the tombs,
Holding one hundred greetings,
And the seven skills of love,
A sword, byword of boldness,
And song, no laughter is left,
Where hand and spade worked to lay
Llywelyn, place for weeping,
Y Moel's son, Môn's not merry,
Handmaids' text of courtly words,
Song's warlock, no weak soldier,
Love's goldsmith and looking-glass.

Deep is the wound to wordcraft,
Deep, if its nightingale's dead.
The world's sadder for his loss,
Cruel trespass in Powys.
Much lamenting in Y Main,
And more above in Mechain,
Penwyn's kin, that he's no more,
Old nightingale of Sulien.
They keen for the cywydd's bard,
Song's widowed now he's buried,
Land's widowed of cywyddau
Without Powys' bow of praise,
Green woods widowed of music,
Love lorn of its alphabet.
No cuckoo or nightingale
Leaves Llwyn-onn for Llanwnnog.
No worthwhile love's still alive,
The blackbird's proud no longer.

Môn's daughters hear the oakwood
Closing over Euron's love.
Cast are thronging thought and song's
Honour beneath green holly,
And Owain's thrush is silent
As a mute in oak and stone,
And Meredudd's author's dead,
The choir's marble conceals him ;
The muse's shield is broken,
Song's master, and smiles have ebbed.
Our Iolo Llywelyn was,
Our Gruffudd or our Dafydd,
Composer of cywyddau,
A heaven-sent bird to men.
He'd shape lyric language like
Honey, or Mary's apples.
Whose now is the sweet tongue's song,
The high bards' Roman Pontiff ?
Where's one word with his passion ?
Where's due deference to art ?
Gone the master, bold wordcraft's
Husband to the house of oak.

Father Griffri, sad constraint,
You carried out Seth's service,
Who came with oil, a lord's share,
From three trees, to his father.
You also brought, gifts of man,
Such an oil to Llywelyn.
You won in the abbey church
Adda Fras' rank and honour,
The man who now lies under
The house altar in his grave.

He too, the lord of our house,
Between lords he was buried.
His body's gone to worship,

Mary's hermit in the choir,
To highest heaven his soul
And with it a new cywydd.
My Lord has invited him
To the feast : his gift, heaven.

SHEEP-DEALING

Two things flow freely on earth,
Water and sun, God sends them,
And the third, lord of learning,
Our kinsman's purse, Corwen's priest.
That three-stringed purse has a way
With us like the tide flowing,
Ebbing when he gives red gold,
Filling for more gold-giving.
The sun's free with fair weather,
More free the wine-giving man.
No miser, never spiteful,
Not mean, except about sheep.

My bargain with Sir Bened
Over sheep cost me his trust.
Through ice and snow they reached me,
Black, white, and branded alike.
And so we went sheep-dealing,
Worse and worse traffic in wares.
I had in this enterprise
Men who were hired to drive them ;
There were two men for herding,
And the third man was the bard.
To Y Rug and Cefn yr Ais
And then to Warwick I drove them,
To England through each clear ford,
Pool to glen to far places.
No dogs went without twenty,

No water left lambs undrowned ;
Missed a fair because of floods,
Night and the streams forbade it ;
Every hedge hindered a third,
Their fleece clung to the fences.
I tried, to no advantage,
Sixty towns to Coventry :
Some of them offered pennies,
Some three and a half for two.
I did not care for the deal,
Twenty sheep dead, bad bargain.

We made for land further on,
York's roads, where fairs were better.
Spent in Lichfield my payment,
Twelve lambs were sold, not enough.
Made for Stafford, a wild land,
Northwards, our language laughed at.
On and on through each foul bush,
Furthest reaches, worst prices.
In selling the ones left us,
Some on time, too late for me,
Some in hand, like interest,
Two lambs, less than a penny.

And he, beneath the rock's edge,
No payment, fair Sir Bened.
There's no return for failure,
He'll not believe how it was.
Profitless for my effort,
A vile sheep-dealer am I.
Losing the tithe distressed me,
God knows Y Cwm's David's cost.
More the wealth in Ardudwy
Than by this business was mine,
Has Tudur, wild rush of song,
Penllyn, in herding wethers.

I had a wretched bargain,
Wretched, but all was not lost.
For me, there's one long-horned sheep,
Pledged, if it comes, a penny.
I'm promised two times over
Silver if I will return.
Could I gain twice the money
In the March, I'd go no more.

A PRIEST'S LOVE

I know how, loving a maid,
A beau behaves, lust's labour :
Fickle man and his fancies,
Love's usury, long for spoils ;
Loving one sweetheart, short-lived,
Then another, fool's notion ;
Today one gay girl in mind,
Another one tomorrow.
If to one, he'd not wed her,
Foolish thing, he fashions song,
He'll likely, lips so gentle,
Sing to the other, gay judge.
Patcher of odes like toll-gates,
The whole thing's for love of spoils.

I know a man, of good stock,
Who loved in truer fashion,
A well-bred saint, wise speaker,
Sir Wiliam, an Abraham,
Trahaearn's heir, fine poet,
David of discerning bards.
My great lord's Merthyr's Mordaf
Where Mary works miracles.
Boundless his yearning to greet
One maiden, Virgin Mary :

She's his love, he'll do no wrong,
Sir Wiliam loves no other.
He's no lover, true temple,
Of a senseless false-faced wench,
But loves the land of banquets
In Tudful, mead-drinking man.
He, God and Mary keep him,
Chaste maid, is dying of love.
He is sending, as Môn knows,
God a host of love's heralds,
A host of, no barren bard,
Prayers to wisdom's author.
To her, fair jewel, he vows
Lovely gems, she's so lovely,
Clear bells, the church put to rights,
Books and relics and crosses.
His office is to greet her
Each day ; he's one with his love.

She'll turn away, God's wonder,
A much-praised man from afar,
Choosing one, the muse's prize,
From her own flock, fine scholar.
No man, were it admitted,
Seemed worthy to her but him.
If there's a lord, firm verdict,
Whom she loves, behold the man !
If a man is a true squire,
He'll seek to join his parish :
If he owns, valiant Urien,
A house he loves, they both go.
God knows if a holy man
Longs for her, he'll pursue her :
If he's wise, we realize,
And liberal, she'll love him.
He's our father, fine mansion,
And pastor, lord of great fame,

Of her comely choir with love
In Tudful, her true poet.

He pledges himself to her
And shapes psalms to her beauty,
Odes of love, undemanding,
Cywyddau of piety.
The cywydd he sings daily,
Well-ordered words, is the Mass.
For love of her, this good man
Knits a song out of syntax.
Rightly, no fault could I find,
Tudful, for Sundays, chose him.
She will ever, by his grace,
Remain with him in Merthyr,
And he is her true lover,
And in heaven they'll keep tryst.

LAMENT FOR SIÔN AP MADOG PILSTWN

My tears flow like a river.
I have wept blood on Siôn's bed.
And thousands weep in Maelor
Harder than a heavy rain.
Gold near the cross and Mary
Begged for Siôn ap Madog's life.
The wretches out there have cried ;
For his sake many fasted.
God paid no heed to wailing,
And would take no gold but him.
Right to fear, face of passion,
A Man who will not be bribed.

This night there's been uprooted
A great oak at Berwyn's base,

P

A hawk of wine-streams stricken,
Like a barren, rootless dream.
The peer of Bwrd and Otwel,
He had Hercules' good luck,
Wrexham's own Alexander
Attending to right and wrong,
Troilus, a second Hector,
Of Trefor and two Maelors.
What role, while Siôn was living,
Had we bards and wanderers
But our hopes of this one man ?
What is it worth, such hoping ?
If war comes by the river,
On the March, or strife in Môn,
I know not, with Pilstwn gone,
Who'll close the gap, who'll save us.

Who'd not bless himself for Siôn ?
Yesterday at home, proudly ;
And today, under the shroud.
I've sown the church with torrents,
Its length and breadth, I've harrowed,
A harrow's teeth in my side.
With sad cry I was tilling :
Under the cross is the ridge.
From God's anger, from vengeance,
Come grave and mattock and spade.
Young men like old are levelled
All too early by the earth.
As if to a vineyard's press
The throng goes to the churchyard.
Men who are youthful and brave
Go early up to heaven,
And some in their middle years,
The noonday of their lifetimes.
Young he was, Owain's kinsman,
To be amidst oak and stone.

Why not bear off a miser,
God, not a bountiful man ?

The son of Rhiwabon is
With saints ; Siôn was an angel.
And sure as Pilstwn was born,
Of his stock there is offspring.
There is a fawn in Maelor,
Stag's son, who'll be a great man,
One here on earth who shall shine,
Hywel the Good's descendant,
A brand from the great embers
That have been all Maelor's light.
In Môn there grows an ashtree
From a noble household's root.
I plead for his father's sake,
Begging God for two favours :
For Siôn and Alswn, heaven,
And splendid growth for their spark.

PETITION

Saint Christopher's sacrifice
Was to bear Christ, bowed double.
And bearing the world's burden
Hercules stood for an hour.
The man in the moon, also,
Bears thorn-faggots, nape to pate.
Through a quarrel, I'm the fourth,
A sick man sorely burdened.

On me, heavy condition,
More weight than eight ancient stones :
Ifan Fychan's frown of wrath,
Like a foe's to its bearer,

Ifan's son, like a mortar,
Adda's grandson, I was his.
Too much for me, my world's scorn,
Ah, the man's back that hoists it !
I've grown weak lugging his wrath,
A lad sallow with sorrow.
Like Samson's, my condition,
Bound to a column of old,
Who in the space of an hour
Pulled the court down upon him.
A lord's the cause, it's dreadful,
My doors fall about my head.
Under a weight, I may fail,
Too much for me I'm stooping.
Mine's the bent back, this I know,
Beseeching reconcilement.
If Ifan's borne me hatred,
I'm ill till I've his good will.

Like a girl when she receives
A greeting's Ifan Fychan :
That one who loves her the best
Is most loathed by a Tegau.
As a hound's pup his master,
So I loved him, Pengwern's stag.

Ifan's achievements made one
Love him more than little men.
Handsome Ifan's lance of steel
Performed the feats of Arthur.
Host in his house to many,
He was chief bard in both arts.
Ifan sings with subtlety,
Nurtures a hundred thousand.
Praise of his house and his voice
And his harp, this is due him :
With a cywydd he is skilled

Gruffudd Gryg, best of singers,
A Llywarch Hen's ode for Gwên,
Nightingale hand of Ifan.
Never such a blameless bard,
Never was Nudd more princely.
No better bard with harpstrings
Was born in many a day.
If it's Ifan sings the song
The young men will be merry.

And I am sad, I'd not wish,
Not for the world, to vex him.
If anger caused half a frown
It weakened me to bear it.
Whatever, noble Welshman,
May do harm to Owain's kin,
I know I am in the wrong :
Confessing wrong brings concord.
Let Ednyfed's daughter ask
Peace for me, I deserve it ;
Young Hywel, stock of Owain,
Is second to her in strength :
To him I'd go, if allowed,
To cast off anger's burden,
And no more frowns from Ifan
On my back for all I'm worth !

THE CITY LIFE

Young, I was one for hillsides ;
Now, nearing man's proper span,
As old age will, it stays put,
My life's led in a city.
When a man's fond of physic
For a cold stomach, milk's bad :
Better for a feeble bard
His pewter dish and bottle.

Mine is the heat of houses,
I'm fond of bread, beer, and meat.
A wooden house in lowlands
Brings me health, like a green tree.
And so I make my dwelling
In the March, I've wine and mead.
A kind, attractive city,
Most blest in its citizens,
Curtain-walled is the castle,
Best of cities, far as Rome !
Croes Oswallt, friend to Jesus,
Great keep for the conqueror.

The London of Owain's land,
Wine-filled homes, land of orchards,
It's a bright and blessed school,
It's a city of preachers ;
Men wise in verse and grammar
Touch God in the fair temple.
The best church, splendid chalice,
Its organ and its bells ;
The best choir, and skilful men,
As far as Canterbury ;
The best band, delightful men,
The men of the white abbey ;
The best of wives, fair their hair
And their gowns, are of Oswallt.
In it there's Cheapside's trading,
And concord, and loyalty.

A tall earl holds this gay place,
He's the best earl in England.
Grace to the town and townsmen,
And God let this refuge last,
Its lords, good place for one's health,
Its commons, its fine yeomen.
With them am I remaining,

Forever their man am I.
My poems could not part with
The town, more than sea the strand.
A burgess I, long marriage :
Pay for it ? Whom should I pay ?
Let Oswallt's townsmen wait for
The payment till I grow hair !
If five pounds made one paymer t,
It's they deserve them, each one.

Where good men were, a bu gess
Was Owain Waed Da in ou land.
The man for his kin only
Sang to pay for his rights.
The same gift is mine to hem,
Here in my hand, like C wain.
A cywydd is my paym nt,
A good song, holdin no spite.
Delight's of no less lue
Than a gold coir a the chest :
Longer lasts, s g by the Welsh,
My name a a words than silver.
I'll spin s g for my brothers,
With t em the men let me stay,
I'll not, without their permit,
Leave them to peddle my songs.

MEDITATION

One high lord here is ruler,
Praising saints in Iâl's great house.
As a judge, he's Bernard's lamb,
A teacher through his poems.
If Dafydd shapes a cywydd,
He makes it Mary's that day.

Shamed is the greedy poet,
Shamed for not shaping such song.

I've sung praise the world over,
Babbling sweet nonsense the while,
Blaspheming since I was six :
He bade me cease such business.
'Be still,' he said, age censured,
'Change like Saul, by praising saints.'
He begged me and he bade me
To give God praise before man,
And to sing, late is the time,
Now to the King of Heaven,
Sharing before life shortened,
Too short is the longest life,
Sharing, paying tithes wisely,
My ageing power with God.
He has shared His gift with us,
Let's give Him proper payment.

Father, Son, Holy Spirit,
God has knowledge of all things,
God of Heaven, Two with Him,
God Himself, undivided.
Good were six words of giving,
God's Son sprung from Mary's womb.
God from virgin soil fashioned
Two people, and gave them the world :
Land, wild, tame, field and forest,
Water, from four elements.
God gave from His torn bosom,
Lanced with steel, His blood for us.
Let us give hearts that are pure
Wholly to him hereafter.

Look on Christ, a lake of blood,
The shape of God, all wounded,

Who will come, Doomsday terror,
To bear our bodies away.
The Father, I know sorrow,
Has inspired three heavy thoughts,
Three swords that cleft me with wounds,
A deep pain as I pondered.
I will die, as is destined,
And I know not at what hour,
I know not what to utter
Not harmful, nor where I'll go.

My holy God, soul's healer,
Of such worth in my sore need,
Subdue my sin and sickness,
Let me die a penitent.
I cry to the Creator,
I shed many tears at night
From love of God and Jesus
And from fear, so just was He,
Fear of the cross on His breast,
The judgment on the rainbow,
Heaven's Eagle, angel ranks,
Fear of the pain that slew Him.
My ears ring with Doom's trumpet
That will call me from my bed :
For what I've done, the payment
Will be laid bare in the scroll.

By the Son and His wonders
There's hope in the upraised host.
The Trinity will listen
To me, in prayer, on high.
My one Saviour, my strong Lord,
Be my refuge on Doomsday,
My shelter, my close of life,
May Heaven be, His dwelling.

OLD AGE

Where are the old men ?   All dead ?
Tonight I am the oldest.
I'm given more than a share
Of old age and bad temper.
I'm a jabbering fellow
Sounding off about old men,
As Rhys Bwtlwng in summer
Sounds on, eloquent boy.
It's asking for each good man
That makes me raise this racket.
Vexing, like one's early verse,
That old fools can't be quiet.
More vexing, if he's not silent,
Caring for the blind all day.

The whole household will witness
How I'm calling from my bed,
Calling, asking for a lord,
From my post, it's my nature,
Each feast day calling a saint,
Calling for Abbot Dafydd.
Though disciplined ones dislike
My role, I'll not be silent.
Much love and the warmth of mead
Make me call for my refuge.
His bright wine and cheerfulness
Cause all the loud commotion.

A foster-father he's been
To me.   May Mary keep him !
My nurse is, while I dwell here,
God's temple that holds his wealth.
Down to his cellar I go,
I go on to his pantry.
Through kind Dafydd I'll go to

Heaven in Iâl's holy land.
Thousands, the more we praise him,
Receive, kind abbot, this food.
A good lord with many bells
Maintains splendid Glyn Egwestl.
The land's weak ones he cares for,
A house he built across Iâl,
A web of stones his breastplate,
Glass and lead his mansion's base.

A bard, I won gold and mead,
Wandered Môn, Gwent, and Gwynedd ;
I wandered nearer, won gold,
Here in Iâl, for my blindness.
Though I am old and fevered,
I'll not whine of weak old age.
If God leaves me this abbot
And two Siôns, I am content.
Siôn Trefor I call a saint,
The seal of the two Powys.
Siôn Edwart I'll not trade for
Two earls ; I visit his home.
Dafydd's court, blessed journey,
At Iâl's another good place.
More and more, like a river,
Honour to him and the Siôns,
The three rulers who prosper,
And the One who blesses them,
The one God, the Father's hosts,
Three and One, in fine concord.

Dafydd ab Edmwnd

A GIRL'S HAIR

Will I win the girl I love ?
And gain the grove of brightness,
Her silk crest like a star in
The sky, her head's golden staves ?
Dragon flame lighting a door,
Three chains like Tewdws Tower,
It flares like a single bush,
From her hair's thatch one bonfire.
A grove of broom or great birch,
Yellow-haired maid of Maelor.
Legion, like hosts of angels,
A many-linked coat of mail,
Pennon of peacock feathers,
High hedge like a golden door,
My girl's hair looks most lovely,
Like a shackle maiden's sun.
All know, should she turn goldsmith,
Whose is the bright splendid hair.

What's round her head in summer
Is something like The Gold Slope.
Crests of grain when they are closed,
A martin's breast, rush peelings,
This lovely growth's the girl's gown,
A tent of sun, like harpstrings.
A peahen bearing always
Hair of broom, down to the ground.
Hard amber interwoven,
Golden grain like chains of twigs,
The bees' work brought to ripeness
Shoots of sunshine from her flesh.
Her hair's a wood, long as trees,

226

A crown of twigs, new beeswax,
Saffron on sprouts of eye-bright,
Cherries like the stars at night.
Well has that crop been sprouting,
Water-grass, gold water-hair.
Urine steeps it like fine herbs,
Grove of silk, the skull's linnet.
Magdalen's sheaf of broom is
The gold crop about her head,
Her loose hair like red-gold reeds,
A dress of gold her tresses.
Her two breasts are entirely
Roofed with gold, twin miracles,
Head with lovely locks laden,
Flax upon a yellow grove.
Gold grove when she spreads it out :
Was ever grove so golden ?

To mark with the chrism of faith
Her head when she was christened,
Life's sun to this grove's given :
None like it beneath the sun.

UNDER THE EAVES

I'm a man walking the night ;
A snug house would be sweeter.
A dull-witted late walker :
May God send the sense to sleep.
The cold night's black about me ;
God save me, the night's so black !
Never small space next a wall
Held one whose face was colder.

Awake, sweetheart, and save me :
God ! there's a wretch next your wall.

Give me, threefold your payment,
Your gown, your alms to the weak,
Your hand to me, your lodging,
Your fair flesh, say that it's mine.
Your courtesy's sweet language,
Your lip like a sip of mead,
Your form, your charm, your laughter,
Your slim brows have ruined me.
Your long hair, bilberry brows,
Your eye dark as your eyebrows,
Your face like friars' vestments,
Black and white, bewitches men,
Your flawless pale complexion,
Two brows black as Brabant cloth,
Your face like snow, night-fallen,
Your blush like a rose bouquet.

Loving you is what I've loved ;
No Saxon's borne such hatred.
I bear your song in anger,
Singing vainly under eaves.
Black rain will have its vengeance,
Soaks my hair, blackens my face.
Hand your kind mother's kerchief
Out the window, roof my head.
I'll bear your song to all lands,
I'll not despair of payment.
I spite myself by loving ;
You're nobly born : so am I.
You are surely well shut in ;
You're beautiful, God keep you.

I bear your song in anger ;
I bear hate : give me a kiss.
Your counsel to curb anger.
Good will be your yielding, dear.

LAMENT FOR SIÔN EOS

Evil for those left behind
Not to speak of the quarrel :
The least wicked of misdeeds
By the best in our language.

O men, were it not wiser,
One slain, no slaying of two ?
It caused, one enemy's blood,
In vengeance, double hatred.
Sad, two splendid men's slaying,
For only a petty cause.
He stabbed the man, no dispute :
His death was not intended.
The fault lay with some of them,
What sprang from a chance mingling.
A dispute about their lives,
Between the two, some friction :
From that, the one man's slaying ;
To avenge it, two men slain.

Though body paid for body,
Better justice for the soul.
There were pledges made later,
His weight in gold for Siôn's life.
I was angered by Y Waun's
Surly law, it stole Eos.
Y Waun, why not under seal
Hywel's law for your Eos ?
When these men put upon him,
In abundance, London's law,
They'd not break, his life at stake,
A cross nor bare a relic.
The man was music's father,
No verdict to let him live

From the twelve, they were as one,
Dear God, about him living.

Song has gone, its green mansions
And wealth forfeit, no Siôn left ;
And heaven's cry follows him,
And schoolless his disciple.
See learning gone to the church;
Where he's lacked, shape your longing.
After Siôn there's no fine art
Of song, nor man who knows it.
An arm broke Eos' tower,
Broken the beat for song's foot,
Broken was descant's schoolroom,
Broken craft, as a string breaks.
Is there from Euas to Môn
Enough skill left to study ?
None has it, even Rheinallt,
Although he plays a man's part.
His fellow has been struck dumb,
Shattered the harp of Teirtud.

You are silent, not a sound,
Golden harp of the harpists.
He'd hold with each nail a string,
Chords for man's voice or bass-note,
Musing with thumb and finger,
Three-fingered treble and mean.
Is there one with Eos gone
His equal at a prelude,
Invention or song for men,
And twined song near a noble ?
In melody, him missing,
Who now could do what he did ?
There's not a man or angel
Who would not weep when he played.

Ah play not the harp tonight,
After the master's sentence.

Heaven heeds not their sentence,
Y Waun's men, against the muse.
Who plays judge will have judgment
From this world to lasting life,
And the same mercy he shows
God the judge freely grants him.
If right the sentence on him,
May they have the same sentence.
His life will still be his own,
Mere change of world, their verdict :
Life for my man in the night,
Life in God for Siôn Eos.

Q

Gwerful Mechain

THE HARP

Gwerful I, of the bankside,
Of Ferry, where silver's loved.
Keeping the Ferry's custom,
A faultless tavern, am I,
Pouring boldly, not mirthful,
In a house, needing a harp.

When I thought, gracious present,
Where I'd gain a horsehair harp,
I sent a plea, free donor,
To Ifan ab Dafydd's home,
A baron bestowing bread,
Barons his two good grandsires.
I was by blood related
To the best men of Y Rhos ;
He's not unkind to kindred,
His cousin, I seek a gift.

A fine gift he'll gladly make,
If kind, complete with horsehair,
With pegs along its full length,
From one end to the other,
The tuner next its corner
With it wherever it goes,
And its neck like those of geese,
And its back full and hollowed.

Here for a cywydd I'll have
A gift, it's Ifan gives it.
And I will give to Ifan
A roast and mead if he'll come,
And welcome when cuckoos sing,
And dinner for two pennies.

A white gown gives sweet welcome
To the men who come with coin.
I'd wish, by men's agreement,
To be faultless to my guests,
To sing sweetly for pleasure
In their midst while pouring mead.

Tudur Penllyn

THE OUTLAW

Fair nights be yours, warm bower,
Tall Kai of green trees and leaves,
You in midsummer, Dafydd,
Roam the woods all the long day.
The strength and grasp of Siancyn,
A stony court, the glen's crag,
Your castle is now the copse,
The dale's oaktrees your towers.
May Nanconwy's stags prosper,
Lasting song, your rank is high.
Most sweet is your skill, Dafydd,
In minstrelsy, exiled stag ;
Outstanding gem, you're handsome,
Every gallant's butterfly.

Your riches are rank and fame,
Grandson of Dafydd Ifor.
A daredevil in warfare
You were judged, and you're no less ;
No finer feat did Roland
Perform than you've done with steel :
When there's song about deeds done,
You're raised above all heroes ;
In every great hall's exploits
Once more you are raised on high.

Are you not Llŷr Llwyd's soldier,
Peacock, for Pembroke, of war ?
You're nephew, Dafydd, bright gem,
To Master Ywain's uncle ;
Nobility's yours by birth,
One of Henry's tall kinsmen.

Honour to you, lasting long,
Was given by Lord Richmond.
From the best forebears you come,
From Rhys Gethin, you're Elffin ;
Absalon in Merioneth,
Sheriff of cuckoo and copse.
Meirig's grandchild, by your birth,
Your grandmother was Cynfyn.

You are the stags' companion,
The Earl's kin, a conqueror ;
And you, the sword of the lords,
Are ruler in our region.
Gwynedd is yours, and peaceful,
You have friends throughout the South.
Beware the towns, wise ruler,
And the towers of that land.
Good is the day's safe-conduct,
Better, Cadell's child, are trees ;
Good are walled town and border,
Best is the glen and grey crag ;
Good was the burgess' pardon,
A shaft for Saxons no worse.

Love the castle of the copse,
Love the soldiers who love you ;
Guard the camp, the woods, the pass,
Your claim to Coed-y-Betws ;
Eight score kinsmen about you,
Eight hundred who love you near,
Eight bands, by Peter, are yours,
Eight woods, and God preserve you.

Gutun Owain

THE HOUNDS

Petition to Hywel ap Rhys on behalf of his nephew, Dafydd ap
Ieuan

A hunter I, hunting hard,
My hunting-ground Mael's mountain.
I'd love to hunt this dawning
A stag over hills with hounds,
Hunt a hind of the region,
Had I the hounds and the land.

To one who's been no miser,
Are there hounds for me to have ?
Two hounds that are sweet-sounding
For Edeirnion's princely hawk.
Hugh of Gwynedd, fair region,
Hywel's the lord of Rhys' line.
He it is who for riches
Is the best man in Y Rug,
The same heart, the same kindness,
Same words as Nudd has our lord.

Three things the baron's fond of,
Falconer, hunt master, hounds,
And I, I've set my heart on
One of these, a gift of hounds.
Two with voices like songbirds,
Two companions in two chains,
They give cry to the master
When they catch wind of the stag.
They proclaim by their fierceness
The sure scent of the fair hind.
Lads holding their heads down low,
Where they go, men come after.

A cry heard down in Annwn
These hounds make in wooded ground.
Song's forged in cuckoo's copses
And death is forged for the fox ;
Well do they, through a valley,
Time their tune trailing a fox.
They stick to a strict measure,
Making music for a hind,
After the hind a carol,
A cywydd after the stag,
Bards of heavenly concord,
Bells of Durham pealing back.

My aim is to have these hounds
From Hywel, a man like Beli.
Let the kind one give Mael's land
These two organs of Gwynedd.
Dafydd, whose hand gives freely,
I'm his nephew, Ieuan's son.
Note of praise, I'm a trader,
Let him trade, nephew am I :
Song for the baron's kinsman,
For his kinsman, his two hounds.

LOVE'S LANGUAGE

Girl of saintly appearance,
O God ! bewitching are you.
You have, a good soul is yours,
The man from Scythia's language,
Clever enchanting image,
Jewel that deceives the just.

Your eye, mocking and merry,
Bright and black, would slay a lad.

I've taken note of signals
You made to me, one or two :
Taking note of a stray glance,
Subtle signs of the forehead,
Reading the slim brows, my dear,
Watching Sunday and feast-day,
Delightful golden writing,
Hint a girl's fond of a lad.
I watch as you are speaking
Like two who have been struck dumb.
None not wise perceives this year
The meanings of our signals.

Let your face send me sweet words
From your heart, none will hear you.
You know how, you are noble,
To speak with sweet courtesy ;
It knows what, this heart of mine,
Your mind is from your manners.
The eyes speak to one who's wise
Sense where none not wise seeks it,
A mirror's slanting turnings,
Thieves finding a place to look.

I'm the one can catch sight of
Each single turn of the eye.
I watch, though I deny it,
You slyly when someone's there :
A sinner's single glimpse of
Heaven before he's in pain ;
Dafydd ap Gwilym's sidelong
Look at Dyddgu, lively girl ;
A lad's look at a sly tryst ;
A hawk's look at a woodcock ;
A thief's look under his brow,
That's the way, at shops' jewels ;

A gentle prisoner's look
Through his cell door at daylight.

My girl, though not once have we
One word of conversation,
We send through the branches' tips
A look, each at the other.
Courtesy speaks a sweet word
Concealed for fear of slander.
Is there one beneath the sky
(There's not !) but me who knows it ?
One deceit, one mockery,
Are we, by God and Mary,
One cunning, one flattery,
One fondness in vain language :
The One and Three, our prayers,
May make the two of us one !

Huw Cae Llwyd

THE CROSS

The Man who stretched on the cross
His span for the world's ages,
Good the place He was given
Above us, His arms spread wide
Over the green land, fair church,
Of Hodni, heaven-honoured,
Where above the nape of stone
God's cross bears Christ in beauty,
And His name plainly inscribed,
Jesus, there in Ystrywaid.
It was like this, says the world,
Friday, after Shrove Tuesday,
With His wounds brightly gleaming,
Heaven's God, stab in His heart.

Three nails were used to martyr
Holy God's hands and His feet.
Both His feet were pinned by one,
A stripe of blood ran down them.
He suffered, such His goodness,
Keen steel hammered through His hand.
Through ribs and robe a blind man
Ripped Him open with a spear.
Three thorn-spikes through his Hair were
Driven to deepen His pain.

I sought to cherish each wound
Upon the Lord of heaven :
No single spot could I find
Unbloody or unbroken.
Who else would act so bravely,
Under heaven, for man's sake ?

His heart and His five wounds were
His pledge to heaven for us ;
Let us then pledge hearts made clean
To Him, let them do homage.
Our sin, if we refuse it
Submission, He will forgive.

Let us go, if we're guilty,
For grace, this Feast of the Cross,
Where He worked, and them wailing,
Many wonders for men's aid,
Restoring full strength to some,
Bringing life back to others.
I breathe a sigh for the spark
Of great wonder that feeds me.
No fool am I for sending
This prayer to gracious God :
That my soul may have brightness,
Holy Son, sanctify me ;
The Blessèd Son's flesh is strong,
Preserve me, Doomsday's Saviour ;
From all cruel wickedness
And pain, protect me ever,
And let my soul never leave
Your country and Your comrades.

The day that brought Jesus back
To life was a fine morning :
For the cripples and the blind,
Those He healed, it was splendid.
May the blood which from His feet
Flowed for us be my refuge ;
From His pierced side I've desired
To have the sweat of Jesus :
But two drops from the passion,
His tears, Who saved me from plague.

God the Father, most of all,
Listen to me, untainted :
I will make, in sacred praise,
The Son a cywydd, call me ;
I will go to the fair feast,
Perfect, unceasing, endless.

Tudur Aled

THE STALLION

Petition to the Abbot of Aberconwy on behalf of Lewis ap Madog

With one who safeguards Gwynedd
I would feast on Conwy's bank,
Abbot over eight districts,
Aberconwy, field of vines,
A lord who gives feasts gladly,
Twice the custom, at his board :
Spices in the one man's dish,
An orange for these others.
Thrice a prince's kitchen's worth,
His cook works hard at turning.

Conwy, in a warm valley,
White stream where I'd have fresh wine,
Wine-rich house, shrine of honey,
Passage and pantry below :
In choosing his wines at once
He was best of all nations,
Glyn Grwst and fair Austin's fort,
Green glen of wine in gallons.
Where seek I saints in session ?
With him and his fellow monks,
Men numbered with the Romans,
White and red the robes they wear.
If his breast and cope were white,
So dressed he'd pass for bishop.
Under minivere he'd pass,
Should he try, as Rome's Pontiff.
Troublesome task, foolish men,
Competing for position :
For the place he won, this man,
Aberconwy, was leader.

243

They'd have a thousand small rents,
He wished the rent of Maenon.
For him on Merioneth's face
A band like woodland blossoms,
Soldiers from Maelor to Rhos,
Tegeingl, his close relations.

Lewis ap Madog's trustful,
Steed begged and bestowed for long,
Choosing by the month of May
Fair girl and steed to bear her.
A stag's form, for a cywydd,
Dimple-nosed, loose in his skin,
Nose that will hold my bridle,
Wide muzzle like a French gun,
Bear's muzzle, jaw in motion,
Bridle's loop holding his nose.
Keen eyes that are like two pears
In his head lively leaping,
Two slender and twitching ears,
Sage leaves beside his forehead.
A glazier's glossed his crupper
As if he polished a gem,
His skin like silk new-woven,
Hair the hue of gossamer,
Silken robe of a skylark,
Camlet upon a young stag.

Like the deer, his eye frenzied,
His feet weaving through wild fire,
He was spinning without hands,
Weaving of silk, moved nearer.
Pursuing the thunder's path
And trotting when he chooses
He loosed a leap at heaven,
Sure of his power to fly.

Stout colt chewing the highway,
A fair-bell, flee from his path !
Stars from the road or lightning
Whenever his fetlocks lift,
Frisky on thirty-two nails,
Sparks they are, every nailhead,
A spinner on a hilltop,
Holds the nailheads to the sun,
Sparks flash from each one of them,
Each hoof sewn with eight stitches.
His vigour I'd compare to
A red hind before the hounds :
His mind was fixed on floating,
A most lively beast he was ;
If driven to the hayfield,
His hoof will not break eight stalks.

He was a river-leaper,
A roebuck's leap from a snake ;
He'd face whatever he wished :
If rafter, try to clear it ;
There's no need, to make him leap,
For steel against his belly.
With a keen horseman, no clod,
He would know his intention.
If he's sent over a fence,
He will run, the lord's stallion,
Bold jumper where thorns grow thick,
Full of spikes, in Llaneurgain.
Best ever, when set running,
Fine steed to steal a fair girl.
Here awaits me a maiden,
Fair girl, if I have a horse.

For a hind's form what payment
Betters praise of the slim foal ?

A PLEA FOR PEACE

The great stags who pour out mead
Are from one shire of Gwynedd.
Old Ynyr's seed, my sworn lord,
My head, may land be Hwmffre's,
Heir of Hywel, the world's lord,
Siencyn's son, and our treasure.
A knight, with blood as noble
As ten earls, a duke are you.
Forfeit this not hereafter
From false counsel, broad-branched oak.

For slandering you and yours
The hindmost yoke stands empty,
Your cousins, I know those men,
In chains, the trees of Ynyr.
These are, of the old bloodline,
Eight of them, men of your blood :
Morgan, the twig of Einon,
Strong Wiliam, spear in his hand,
Two of the same flesh as Siencyn,
Derwas' two roses of gold ;
Tudur Fychan, the land's shield,
Derwas' bull, his feet gilded ;
Seven cousins I'd not put,
Siôn's son Siencyn, before him ;
Hywel, his kinsman was there,
Fychan, dragon of Mechain,
His Siôn, who has noble roots ;
And Wmffre, jewelled bridle ;
Brave Gruffudd, stag of keen steel,
Of Iefan's blood and Dafydd's ;
Morgan Siôn, full of welcome,
Of Penllyn, spear swift and keen.

Strong your kind, like rooted oaks,
And the oak grove's uprooted.

And where have there been such trees
That should embrace each other ?
To fell, like Brutus, a house
Is simpler than to raise it.
Ynyr of Nannau's offspring,
It's our woe, if you grow weak.

Dear God ! why should men be vexed
By some slanderer's malice ?
Blood feuds, by a feeble cause,
Led to conflict at Camlan.
Three futile frays through hatred,
Ancient follies, many slain :
Battle begun by a pup ;
Sad deed, Arderydd's action ;
More wicked Mordred's treason,
How he provoked, for two nuts,
Strife once more by two shepherds,
Because of some skylark's chicks.

Men hate each other like this,
At present, for positions :
Once, ousting men was hated,
Today, pity settled men !
I can find here no friendship,
Not a man to plead for good ;
Trusted, truly, not a one
Except the man who's two-faced ;
What's wicked today is truth,
To the good none will listen.

Our leaders had no need of
Their resorting to the lords :
Though you give them gold today
You'll not rule in your lifetime.
If there's wrath between Rhos' buds,
See if there is good reason :

R

No foreigner is able,
This you can do for yourselves.
Harm and hatred, from losses,
Peacemakers, once, could dissolve :
Nothing, this generation,
Through anger, but squandered wealth.
No good comes of the expense,
But devilish wrongdoing.

Wales is worse by this stripping,
England's bettered by our taint.
A hundred bills burden us —
Christ's cross, shield us from sessions !
One kinsman blames another,
Easily this hand blames that.
Let each strip, sift, untruthful,
The other's fault, it's believed :
Word of wrongdoing lingers,
Many times staining blood kin ;
This one's shamed, not the other :
Truth told, it's the other's fault.
It is best to bear the dark
Hurtful word, not deny it.
Stop an arrow, no dispute,
Once it has left the bowstring !

No joy to us, unseemly,
And you so many, to chide.
Wisdom should come, splendid clan,
From folly, and bard's frankness.
The scroll I hold shows a wheel
And a face at its centre ;
Notice there, on the wheel's rim,
Four true words, never ending :
Peace, the world's pulse of power,
It is this, then, that breeds wealth ;
Proud wealth, I know the wheel,

When it is strong, breeds warfare ;
Warfare breeds a misery,
Want, from anger and anguish ;
Want, to unhappy wretches,
When it's widely spread, breeds peace.
These words are on the wheel's edge,
Could any recognize them.
Man's rise, he'll not stay below,
And fall is on this circle.
If it turn once to mischance,
God ! no return to fortune.

Here were two noble houses ;
Over a clash, Hwmffre's vexed.
Making peace on high today
Atop the wheel would keep you :
Let its rim rise, God shields you ;
Allow all your blood to rise,
Trees should bear leaves together,
Safeguard the trees at your side ;
The grove, would all were pleasant,
Is a grim grove without love.
Men higher than a gold seal
Sharing a noble lineage,
Despite frowns, sparing what's theirs,
Out of a frown make friendship.
Never lived one not kindly
Because so clean are their hearts :
Let there be peace, agreeing,
Had five thousand men been slain.

An alms it were, no one slain,
Unstained to plead for union.
If your long wrath has chilled you,
Grace blazes at once with warmth :
Noble blood that was frozen,
Melt those of your blood towards you ;

Today may there be water
Under the ice, thin and cold.
Draw poison from your true blood,
The sweet blood's scent is honeyed.
Have sense, heart-rending your strife,
And set good sense above you.
Take no note of injuries,
Amendment and denial :
If you're kind, like your father,
Amends, denial, you'll make.

Between you, on your kinsmen,
With all grace, work miracles.
By the spear and dear Jesus,
By His pain for Lazarus,
May the Three bring agreement
By Mary's tears for her Son.

LOVE'S FRUSTRATION

My passion for Iseult's twin
Went worse than a wild arrow.
Loving a maiden's image
Is as hard as toting stone.

Twin of Gwenedydd and Non,
A sister to the Virgins,
Your name has enrolled one more
With the eleven thousand.
Heed one who's weak, cheeks wasting,
From your hue, my gold-browed dear :
Because gold grows on your crown
Your blushing is so lovely ;
Your complexion makes you proud,
See yourself in the mirror,
Hold your image in the glass —
God is the one devised it.

So slim is your cinctured waist
You could spin in my handspan.
God, there's no church, noble girl,
Not empty if you're absent.
O God, the church was crowded
If only your face were there !
Why need I, clear face, a glass,
Since you're foolish, to glimpse you ?
No sweetness, under the stars,
The same as you, fair maiden.
No girl drives me to suffer
In wind and water but you.
Coming from the far corners
Over land, how hard it was :
You would not, at journey's end,
Step once across the threshold.

God ! how gentle your gesture,
A gentleness filled with stone.
My life, my affliction speaks,
In two places of darkness,
Your bright eyes, two youthful hues,
You struck, dear, with your hatred.
Your arms, at last, above me,
Be the angels of my bed !
Precious they are, your kisses,
For man's health he'd not have two :
You'd not give one, for life's need ;
Sell some, by Him who made you !

Auburn your brows, white your hand,
White is your cheek and wine-stained.
Fair one, the pain you cause me
Eight-plated steel could not bear.
Into the grave should enter
One with half my sleeplessness.

I lie on one side, sleepless,
A bird's sleep, tonight, is mine,
The sleep of fish in the sea
Reclining in rough water.
More in one night I tremble
Than the aspen does in eight.
Your hue held in mind, in sleep,
Turns me away from slumber.
The world finds me a byword,
And never a pang have you.

To have you, at the grave's edge,
I'm no man, merely wastage,
This is my only longing,
Though improper, my pure soul.
Scarcer you make your speeches,
Stronger my long sickness grows.

No nearer I, so thwarted,
One step, for this, than thief saint,
Waiting near you seven eves,
Seven excuses to see you.
Unwise, one who's not silent,
And wise are you, keeping still.
I could have no happy life,
Nor fail one night to greet you.
No more of words so distant,
In mercy, a better word :
I beg of you, my seagull,
Sentence me soon — life, or death.

Wiliam Llŷn

LAMENT FOR SIR OWAIN AP GWILYM

Heavy on ice, drifted snow :
Heavier a bond broken.
What you pledged me in a glade
Was like a maiden's promise.

I'm vexed, song's foremost shaper,
Sir Owain, fair star of song.
Do you recall, I complain,
The triple pact between us,
To stroll amid gold and mead,
To sing to Gwynedd's daughters,
From Llŷn to Tywyn, we two,
From Tywyn to the southland ?

I've gone, I go, to seek you
To the house at Tal-y-llyn,
And there a spear of grief pierced
My side : I did not see you.
I called to you, Gwilym's son,
A shrill call, and heard nothing.
Faithful grove, prophet's orchard,
Spear of speech, where do you stay ?
Is it the South, source of mead,
Gifted angel, or Gwynedd ?
The tryst was like a troth-day,
And I swear you did not come.
Tell me, you are well-mannered,
Household bard, who hindered you ?

'By God, dusky grasping death,
The great foe of all mortals,
He held my feet and my hands,
I could not turn to go there.

The fair skin, like a harvest,
Is turning black in the earth.
The lips that have plaited praise
Are silent in the gravel.'

Sir Owain, I am stricken,
Skilful speech, if you are there.
If for proud wealth, hawk of wine,
You're held, Austin-like teacher,
Ask of God, fair and gentle
His name, to take wealth instead.

'I'll not do so, I'll not plead
To God, silence is better.
Worldly wealth is not able
To lengthen man's life one hour.
Dullard, think this about life :
God rules how long's a lifetime.'

That is true, noteworthy man,
To think upon it grieves me.
Come, three languages' flower,
Now, if you may, from the grave.
Unless you come, long-lived oak,
Farewell fine feats of music.
None will seek, stag not hunted,
The huntsman or hawk or hounds.
No girl's love, no courtship vow,
No praise, no maiden's laughter.
The greenwood's broad-branching trees
May not bear leaves hereafter.
Love's reaches, achievement's worse,
Falling the hall of friendship.
God took, like a dread mistake,
A strong stag, kind, wise, merry.
Slain the court's eye and limb,

Song-gear's support and handmaul.
Wise master, in earth's the best
Hind ox ever of altars.

If there's love amid kinsmen,
None has lived with lips like these.
If two lands came to contend
For song's name and dwelling place,
Gold today would be given
Like snowflakes for you to live.
Strongly you rhymed rich lyric
Over the yoke, song's hind ox.
Vain is the yoke, the couple,
The gold chain, since you lay down.
Cold is ice on a roadway,
Colder my bruised breast, you gone.

Farewell, pure and noble flesh.
It's time for me, Sir Owain,
To take leave without redress,
And hard it is to leave you.
Bard, if below in the grave
You stay, to lie there always,
In the earth, sad fate's demand,
Learning will dwell forever.

Siôn Tudur

THE BARDS

Shamed, the world says, we poets !
And shamed the state of our craft !
The role of bard lacks honour ;
It was once renowned, not scorned :
Praising God, before others,
Full, frequent, unpaid-for praise ;
Praising the blood of thousands,
Princes and swift-riding knights ;
Lords of the scent of learning,
Mighty bishops in our midst ;
Fruitful, generous chieftains,
Bearers of the ancient blood ;
Chieftains and priests of the faith,
Prelates, luck of their regions.
Some were summoned as rulers,
By their wisdom, by men's wish :
Right to, deep erudition,
Love learning for love of God.
Right for a bard, handsome man,
To pour praise on a warrior,
Because the wastrel would not
Venture his life in the fray.

We poets make, such wretches,
Of gardeners men of rank,
Giving too fine a lineage,
Praising Jack as well as John,
Each helter-skelter stealing
The stanzas of splendid bards,
Remodelled for low wretches,
Bribed labour, like painting crows.

A plume from each bright-cloaked bird
Would make the crow's breast brilliant.
A naked churl, no true man,
A crown would make him kingly.
A tinker gives us silver :
He'll have lordly lines, fine scroll.
With office, two stern emblems,
He'll pass for noble with ease.
Through extortion, shrewd business,
Through usury, others squeezed,
He'll raise a broad-lawned manor,
Lock tightly his fine white house.
Easier to, good bailiff,
Break one's neck where he stays hid,
Than, any day, for hungry
Men to break fast in his hall.
In courtesy he's lacking,
The man begrudges his gold.
Scant hearing, bread, watered milk,
Plain buttermilk he'll give them.
Though he'd not feed the frail,
Nor hand alms to the needy,
Not a penny if he's hanged,
I'm well-paid for fine lineage.

Chart from the bard's hand decks him,
The bard's hand has done much wrong,
Stealing pedigrees and arms
From stately men for stinking.
He's a bore, the land over,
Bragging of lines, arms, and land,
And a botched scroll of forebears,
And scabby badge in pinched pouch.
Slap-dash we gave him his arms :
His dad's arms, a dung-shovel.
If one looks for truth, no lie,
His coat of arms is shaky.

World-wide, all across the globe,
They've climbed up from the gutter.
Who climbs, for all his hoarding,
Sudden chance, he falls with ease.
A beetle flies above roads,
He's in dung before daybreak.

Every churl would employ us :
Let's quit, we should see our crime.
Unless we change our ways now
The world will not respect us.
God keep us from praise-shaping
For those unfit for shaped praise.
I'd sing from the bench marvels
For those men deserving fame.
I would sing and study praise
For proper men, right-living,
Letting, what's fit held firmly,
A base man be labelled base.
A prince is a prince always,
A prince will be known as prince,
Eagle as eagle, high-ranked,
And crow as crow, no higher,
Hawk of noble hawk's lineage,
And a kite ever a kite.
In Siôn's purse, do what they will,
No gold from churls hereafter.

THE NAG

My bay horse with tossing mane,
Lively at need, staid fellow,
You've munched my oats and fodder,
You've munched and have had your fill.

Steadily, now, be stirring
To do something, precious bay :
Bear a bard near Carmarthen,
When asked, to win gold and wine,
To Saint David's wise Bishop's
Palace, an unswerving path,
Abergwili, best hearthside,
Bards' harbour, their meat and drink.
I've craved, in a cosy niche,
A warm feast from Lord Rhisiart.

'Silence, Siôn, greedy fellow,
Your fervent tale, you're a wretch.
I'm weak-kneed, stumbling, clumsy,
Sorry head and heavy tail.
I groan that I get no food
And no shoes, you've no kindness ;
If I'm lean, it's lack of oats,
Lack of fodder and leisure.
You caught my rash, foolish eye ;
On my back you did badly :
Heaving, you hurt my crupper,
Bad luck to your cap and gear !
Your spur, you're a fat fellow,
Was a goad to skin and ribs.
You've raked my rear to the bone,
From your bare blade, eight gouges.
Sad steed from toting maidens,
A slow runner on a slope !
Hard days in Denbigh for me,
All night, frolic and faintness :
You've wine in your mouth, and mead,
And I, my teeth for chomping !
You stay always, disgraceful,
For three days and for three nights :
Each steed has his fill of oats,
And I have my nose bridled !

Mine's a great wait, so delayed,
With lean ribs, for the cuckoo.

'I'll not leave here for Dyfi
And Bwlch y Groes, while you live.
If you'll make, though, the effort,
A wincing old nag's advice,
Go to the place I desire,
Through the water to Gwydir.
Sing loudly, and to the harp,
Of your great love for Morys,
And freely to you he'd give
A colt, if you but fetch it.'

Tomos Prys

THE PORPOISE

Fair nimble keen-edged porpoise
Leaping lovely waves at will,
Seacalf, brow strangely shaded,
Smooth the way, strange-sounding lad.
Glad you are to be noticed,
Gay on wavecrests near the shore,
A fierce-looking cold-framed head,
Bear's face in frigid currents.
He skips, he shakes like ague,
And then he waggles away,
Black mushroom, wrestles the sea,
Staring at it and snorting.
You are ploughing the breaking
Crests of the waves of the sea ;
You split the salty ocean,
Are in the heart of the wave,
Daring shadow, swift and clean,
Skull of the sea, strand's pillion.
He hoes waves, water viper,
His looks give the heart a fright.
You're white-bellied, quite gentle,
Rover of the captive flood.
Boar of the brine, deed of daring,
He roams the sea, long bright trail.
Summers, when weather changes,
You come rocking before storms,
Fierce boar, wild infernal churn,
On wild tides cross and greedy.
Lance with gold-crested breastplate,
Fish in a closely-clasped coat,
Sea's burden, tress on bosom,
He slides, holds on a wave's slope.

Sea's saddle, take your bearing,
Find a path to the fierce brine.
Choose a fathom, go for me,
Steady memory's envoy.
Take a trip, from Menai's bank,
On a sure course for Lisbon,
And then swim in a moment
To Spain's border, the world's breast.
Search along the water's edge,
Great his fame, for a warrior,
Pyrs Gruffudd (are hearts not sad ?),
Trust's pearl, heart pure and faithful,
Honour of Penrhyn, sound branch,
Gentle lord, who more manly ?

It's six years, O how weary,
Since he went abroad by ship
To seas beyond the inlet,
Cross the bar, across the world.
Is it not high time he left
The salt water, kind hero,
And came, relief of worry,
To his court from that foul place,
And lingered where he's longed for,
And made all his people glad ?

When you see him, fine labour,
Very bold aboard his ship,
Call to him, bright his harness,
The petition that you bring,
And greet him, fruitful task,
With much song from his comrade,
Sweetly, a man who once went
Sailing on the same voyage
Till he, cheerful admission,
Purchased wisdom when he waned :
Then truly he discarded
The ocean and all its ways.

Well-designed is your dwelling,
A hide-out from terriers.

Sorry scheme, you live yonder,
Paunchy lad, by plundering,
Pilfering, when it's quiet,
And strolling through leaves all day :
Kid's meat, when it's to be had,
Ewes, if they're for the taking ;
A fine life, when there are lambs,
Blameless for you to tithe them.
Take hereafter, yours freely,
A goose and hen, unrebuked :
Clever you are, bird-snatching,
Hillside or bog, wild and tame.

All accomplishments your gift,
When closed in, you're a lion.
And if you come with twilight
Is there one so full of sense,
Or any with tricks slicker
Than yours, savage-snarling fox ?
Nowhere, I know, in the grove,
Will I find shrewder judgment.
I am a man unwelcomed,
Disheartened, speechless, unloved,
No malice, no violence,
Strengthless in every struggle :
Yours, today, well-earned honours,
Teach me, a gift, how to live ;
If you will give good counsel,
Forever I'll sing your praise.

'Be still, sound man, no clamour,
No search for help, no complaint.
See that there are, and take heed,
Two paths for your protection :

One true path, straight is its course ;
Another one through falsehood.

'Seeking success, preferment ?
I'd wish you to live like me.
One who's simple and peaceful,
Without malice, he'll not mount,
And integrity today,
In the world's view, is foolish.
Pillage or hazard the world,
Try cunning for the moment ;
Learn to keep watch, look for faults,
Spare not one nor the other.
Remember, basic lesson,
Remember gain, the world's rule.
Devise, beware of a frown,
Traps for all, know all evil.
Do a kindness to no one
All your life, lest life be lost.
Make yourself known where you go,
From fear, cause much gift-giving.

'Hard to live, no denying,
Today by what's gained from love.
If you wish to live for long,
Go with praise, learn to flatter,
And by lauding each small thing
Learn the art of deception.
Speak sweetly on each errand,
Let no profit slip your hand.
Speak nothing but pious words,
Your malice in your belly.
Let not a man who's been born
Know any place your purpose :
That's the way a fool is known,
He reveals what he's thinking.
To prey on the weak's the way ;

Treat the strong with smooth talking.
Do wrong, make no amendment :
To you, man, a good day comes.
Do all this, you'll not founder,
With deception as your guide.

'I have nothing more to tell :
The other path, consider.
I see the hounds in pursuit,
Hard for me to speak further
Or stay here on the hillside.
Farewell, I must flee above.'

Siôn Phylip

THE SEAGULL

Fair gull on the water's bank,
Bright-plumed breast, well-provided,
Hawk does not seize or pursue,
Water drown, nor man own you.
Nun feasting on the ocean,
Green sea's corners' coarse-voiced girl,
Thrusting wide through the lake's neck,
And then shaking a herring,
Salt water's clear white sunlight,
You're the banner of the shore.
The blessed godchild are you,
Below the bank, of Neptune :
A sorrow for you, the change
Of your life, cold your christening,
Brave white bird in rough waters,
Once a girl in a man's arms.

Halcyon, fair slim-browed maiden,
You were called in your kind land,
And after your man, good cause,
To the waves then you ventured,
And to the wild strait's seagull
You were changed, weak-footed bird.
You live, quick fish-feeding girl,
Below the slope and billows,
And the same cry for your mate
You screech loudly till doomsday.

Was there ever on the sea
A more submissive swimmer ?
Hear my cry, wise and white-cloaked,
The hurt of the bare sea's bard :

268

My breast is pained with passion,
Pining for love of a girl.
I have begged from my boyhood
That she'd make one tryst with me,
And the tryst was for today :
Great was grief, it was wasted.
Swim, forget not my complaint,
To the dear maiden's region ;
Fly to the shore, brave brightness,
And say where I was held fast
By the mouth, no gentle wave,
Of rough Bermo, cold foaming,
In all moods a sorry spot,
A cold black sea for sailing.

I rose, I travelled as day was
Breaking towards that dear bright face.
Dawn came on a thorny seastrand,
A cold day from the south-east.
A foul wind winnowed gravel,
Stripping stones, the whirlwind's nest.
The signs grew darker with dawn,
Twrch Trwydd drenching the beaches.
Inky was the wind's gullet
Where the western wind draws breath.

Harsh is the shore in conflict
If the western inlet's rough :
The sea spews, turning rocks green,
From the east spews fresh water.
Deep heaves from the ocean-bed,
In pain the pale moon's swooning.
The green pond is heaved abroad,
A snake's heave, sick from surfeit.
Sad heave where I saw tide ebb,
Rain's drivel that came pouring,

Cold black bed between two slopes,
Salt-filled briny sea-water.
Furnace dregs, draff of hell-spit,
Mouth sucking drops from the stars,
A winter night's greedy mouth,
Greed on the face of night-time,
Crock-shaped wet-edged enclosure,
A ban between bard and girl,
Foul hollow gap, raging pit,
Foggy land's filthy cranny,
Cromlech of every sickness,
Narrow pit of the world's plagues.
That pit was the sea-pool's haunt,
High it leaped, pool of prickles.
As high as the shelf it climbs,
Spew of the storm-path's anguish.
It never ebbs, will not turn :
I could not cross the current.

Three waters could flow eastwards,
Three oceans, these are the ones :
The Euxin, where rain wets us,
The Adriatic, black look,
The flood that runs to Rhuddallt,
Ancient Noah's flood turned salt.
The water-gate at Bermo,
Tide and shelf, may it turn land !

NOTES

AFTER the title of each poem I have listed first the text on which the translation is based. Other texts are listed when I have adopted some of their readings or am indebted to their annotation, but I have not attempted to discuss variant readings in these notes nor to offer solutions to ambiguous phrases or passages.

The following abbreviations are used for the anthologies most frequently cited :

BYU : *Barddoniaeth Yr Uchelwyr*, edited by D. J. Bowen (Cardiff, 1959).

DGG : *Cywyddau Dafydd ap Gwilym a'i Gyfoeswyr*, edited by Thomas Roberts and Ifor Williams (Cardiff, 1935).

IGE : *Cywyddau Iolo Goch ac Eraill*, edited by Henry Lewis, Thomas Roberts, and Ifor Williams (Cardiff, 1937).

OBWV : *The Oxford Book of Welsh Verse*, edited by Thomas Parry (Oxford, 1962).

Names of persons and places and some unfamiliar words are to be found in the glossary, but when a poem required much genealogical information I have supplied it in the notes.

Very little is known in most cases of the poets' lives, and I have supplied biographical information only when it seemed useful.

Quotations from *The Mabinogion* in the notes and the glossary are from the translation by Gwyn Jones and Thomas Jones (London, 1949).

DAFYDD AP GWILYM. He was born *c.* 1320, probably at Brogynin in Cardiganshire, died *c.* 1380, and was buried at Strata Florida. He was a member of one of the most important families in South Wales during the fourteenth century ; his uncle, Llywelyn ap Gwilym, was Sub-Constable of Newcastle Emlyn in 1343. Very little is known of his life, though the poems have caused much biographical speculation : these show, at least, that he travelled widely through Wales, and had a considerable acquaintance with noblemen and bards, as well as women, in many regions.

I must stress that no chronological ordering of Dafydd's poems is possible, and therefore the sequence in which I have arranged them is quite arbitrary, intended simply as a means of entertaining the reader who wishes to read straight through the selection. It is the Morfudd poems that tease one with

271

the possibilities of a chronological order, and that would gain much if such an order could be established (just as a chronological reading of Catullus's Lesbia poems gives the sense of a full lyrical exploration of the stages of a relationship, of a whole greater than the sum of its parts).

All of the translations are based on *Gwaith Dafydd ap Gwilym*, edited by Thomas Parry (Cardiff, 1952) ; the numbers after the titles refer to this text.

The Seagull, 118.

In a Tavern, 124.

A Celebration of Summer, 27.

cauldron of Annwn : the cauldron of rebirth in Celtic myth.
Ifor Hael, 7.

The Girls of Llanbadarn, 48.

The Owl, 26.

The Girl of Eithinfynydd, 57.

A Stubborn Girl, 41.

The Rattle Bag, 125.

The bag was used to frighten wild animals away from the sheep ; it was made of hide, filled with stones, and carried on a pole.

Gilding the Lily, 49.

Under the Eaves, 89.

The Grey Friar, 137.

This is the only poem in the book that is not a *cywydd* ; it is a *traethodl*, which employs couplets with two unstressed rhymes as well as the *cywydd* rhyme pattern and may be the form from which the *cywydd* evolved. My translation uses some couplets of two unstressed endings and one of two stressed along with the *cywydd* pattern of line-endings used in the other poems.

three excepted : Adam, Eve, and Melchisadech is the usual interpretation.

The Holly Grove, 29.

lavish Robert : identity unknown.

The Coward, 58.

The Dream, 39.

Morfudd's Arms, 53.

Morfudd's Oath, 43.

The Wave, 71.

The Mass of the Grove, 122.

A Garland of Peacock Feathers, 32.

Virgil's fairs : Virgil was generally thought of in the Middle Ages as a magician ; Dafydd is referring to magic shows at fairs.

Betrayal, 85.

The World's Brittleness, 76.

Lament for Gruffudd ab Adda, 18.

like a goose : a goose was killed by splitting its head. 'Boorish' is meant to have its full social force, adding its weight to the simile : this way of dying was not worthy of a nobleman.

The Shadow, 141.

Dyddgu, 45.

Her complexion : 'On the morrow early [Peredur] arose, and when he came outside, a fall of snow had come down the night before. And a wild she-hawk had killed a duck ... and a raven alighted on the bird's flesh. Peredur stood and likened the exceeding blackness of the raven, and the whiteness of the snow, and the redness of the blood, to the hair of the woman he loved best, which was black as jet, and her flesh to the whiteness of the snow, and the redness of the blood in the white snow to the two red spots in the cheeks of the woman he loved best.' 'Peredur', *The Mabinogion*, p. 199.

Love's Shaft, 111.

Noah's psalm : Dr. Parry suggests that Dafydd may have been watching a miracle play about the Deluge.

The Mist, 68.

The Mirror, 105.

A Gift of Wine, 128.

An Invitation to Dyddgu, 119.

Four Women, 98.

Summer, 24.

A *cywydd* that demonstrates Dafydd's technical dexterity by ending each couplet with 'haf' ('summer') and thus employing only one rhyme throughout.

Love's Fever, 102.

The original gives still another demonstration of skill by its use of *cymeriad* (correspondence) : each line begins with 'H'. I have not attempted to match this feat in the translation.

The Wind, 117.

A Prayer to St. Dwyn, 94.

The Birch Hat, 59.

A Moonlit Night, 70.

The Three Porters, 80.

A Wish for Eiddig, 75.

    let a foe's zeal : if Eiddig must come home, let it be as a corpse.

Aubade, 129.

The Star, 67.

May and January, 69.

The Skylark, 114.

The Judgment, 106.

The Sword, 143.

    twirling taper : 'buarth baban', a flaming stick that was whirled in a circle to amuse a child.

The Rival, 54.

A Simile for Morfudd, 42.

Morfudd's Fickleness, 93.

    the Black Idler : 'y Du Segur', possibly Eiddig again, who is called 'y du ffraeth' in 'A Wish for Eiddig'. 'Du' ('black') is a word frequently applied to the husband by the bards in love poems.

Morfudd and Dyddgu, 79.

Love in Secret, 74.

Beauty's Ruin, 81.

The Magpie, 63.

Morfudd Grown Old, 139.

The Ruin, 144.

The End of Love, 90.

GRUFFUDD AB ADDA, *fl.*1340–70.   A bard of Powys Wenwynwyn, killed in the manner described in Dafydd ap Gwilym's elegy for him.

The Maypole.   *OBWV* 54, *DGG* lxv.

The Thief of Love.   *DGG* lxvi.

MADOG BENFRAS, *fl.*1340–70.

The Saltman.   *OBWV* 48, *DGG* lxx.

LLYWELYN GOCH AP MEURIG HEN, *fl.*1360–90.

The Skull.   *DGG* lxxxvii.

The Coal-Tit.   *OBWV* 50.

Lament for Lleucu Llwyd. *OBWV* 49, *DGG* lxxxviii.
The Snow. *DGG* lxxxv.

GRUFFUDD GRYG, *fl.*1360–1400.
The April Moon. *OBWV* 56, *DGG* lxxiv.
The bard's pilgrimage to the shrine of St. James at Com-
postella in Spain is delayed by the weather.
Harry's shore : England. The king is Henry IV.
twirling taper : see the note on Dafydd ap Gwilym's 'The
Sword'.
his bounty : the gifts for the shrine.
Lament for Rhys ap Tudur. *DGG* lxxx.
Richard : King Richard II.
Dafydd's Wounds. Parry, *Gwaith Dafydd ap Gwilym*, 147.
This is the first poem of a bardic contention between the two
poets.
The Fickle Girl. *DGG* lxxiii.
the course that one man : a proverbial example of how not to
catch a cow. The girl has been foolish to break with him
before she is sure of happiness with her new lover.
The Yew-Tree. *OBWV* 55, *DGG* lxxxii.
Saintly Dafydd : 'Dafydd llwyd', which might be a proper
name. Unless 'llwyd' is interpreted as 'pale' or 'grey', it
seems unlikely that it refers to Dafydd ap Gwilym.
Christ the King. *BYU* 2.

IOLO GOCH, *c.* 1320–*c.* 1398.
Sir Hywel of the Axe. *IGE* ix.
When greed's reward : The French king was captured in the
battle of Poitiers, 1356, by the Black Prince.
Sycharth. *OBWV* 51, *IGE* xiii.
The Ploughman. *OBWV* 53, *IGE* xxvii.
Portrait of a Maiden. *IGE* i.
The Ship. *IGE* xxv.
Bard and Beard. *IGE* ii.
Irish : often used by the bards as an insulting adjective.
Lament for Dafydd ap Gwilym. Parry, *Gwaith Dafydd ap
Gwilym*, p. 422 ; *IGE* xiv.

GRUFFUDD LLWYD, *fl.*1380–1410.
Morgannwg. *IGE* l.

POEMS OF UNKNOWN OR UNCERTAIN AUTHORSHIP.

A number of these were formerly attributed to Dafydd ap Gwilym, but are excluded from Dr. Parry's edition of Dafydd's works. The possibility of Dafydd's authorship of at least the first three poems is still a matter of scholarly debate, in which I have neither the ability nor the wish to take part. 'The Virgin Mary' was at one time attributed to Iolo Goch ; 'A Visit to Flint' has been claimed for both Lewis Glyn Cothi and Tudur Penllyn ; 'Lent' is often assigned to the fifteenth-century poet Bedo Aeddrem.

The Snow. *BYU* 24.

The Grove of Broom. *BYU* 25, *OBWV* 63.

In Dyfed : 'And as they were sitting thus, lo, a peal of thunder, and with the magnitude of the peal, lo, a fall of mist coming, so that no one of them could see the other. And after the mist, lo, every place filled with light. And when they looked the way they were wont before that to see the flocks and the herds and the dwellings, no manner of thing could they see.' 'Manawydan Son of Llŷr', *The Mabinogion*, p. 43.

The Stars. *OBWV* 64, *DGG* xl.

Bright scales : 'And in that place [Lludd] had a pit dug in the ground, and in that pit he set a tub of the best mead that might be made, and a covering of silk over the face of it, and he himself keeping watch that night. And as he was thus, he saw the dragons fighting, and when they were worn and weary they descended on top of the covering, and dragged it with them to the bottom of the tub. And when they had made an end of drinking the mead they fell asleep. And in their sleep Lludd wrapped the covering about them, and in the safest place he found in Eryri he hid them in a stone coffer.' 'Lludd and Llefelys', *The Mabinogion*, p. 93.

The Swan. *BYU* 28.

her name : Dwyn.

The Tryst. *BYU* 35, *DGG* xxi.

The last four lines are omitted from *BYU* : Mr. Bowen believes that they are a spurious addition, since they are found in other poems. I have retained them because they make a very effective ending to the poem : if a later poet or copyist added them, it was with an awareness of the improvement they give to the poem as a whole.

The Jealous Husband. *BYU* 31.

Irishman : not meant literally ; the term is an insult.

the soil and rod : the measuring rod, which was buried with the body.

Love's Architect. *BYU* 29.

The Virgin Mary. *IGE* xxxi.

Ave : a frequent medieval comment, that Ave reversed the letters of Eva, as a sign that Mary undid the harm done by Eve.

The Salmon. *DGG* xxix.

The Nun. *BYU* 30.

A Visit to Flint. *BYU* 23.

Lent. Gwyn Williams, ed., *The Burning Tree*, 32 ; Robert Stephen, ed., *The Poetical Works of Bedo Aeddrem, Bedo Brwynllys, and Bedo Phylip Bach* (M.A. thesis, National Library of Wales, 1907), p. 245.

SIÔN CENT, *fl.*1400–30.

The Bards. *IGE* lx.

The poem is one from a contention with Rhys Goch Eryri, the 'old man' referred to in the opening lines.

Thomas Lombard : the identity of the books referred to in the following lines is uncertain.

The Purse. *IGE* lxxxvi.

The attribution of this poem to Siôn Cent has been questioned, but the use of a refrain, rare in the *cywydd*, is found in some of his other poems and strengthens the case for his authorship.

Repentance. *BYU* 4.

foul marshes : hell, as it is often conceived in the age.

The Vanity of the World. *OBWV* 58, *IGE* xcvi.

LLYWELYN AP Y MOEL. Died 1440.

The Wood of the Grey Crag. *BYU* 15.

The Battle of Waun Gaseg. *OBWV* 57, *IGE* lxiii.

LEWIS GLYN COTHI, *fl.*1447–86. He supported the Lancastrians and Jasper Tudor in the Wars of the Roses, and was outlawed in 1461 because of it. It is said that his eviction from Chester, referred to in the first two poems, was caused by his marriage to a widow of that city without the consent of the burgesses.

The Sword. E. D. Jones, ed., *Gwaith Lewis Glyn Cothi*, vol. i (Aberystwyth and Cardiff, 1953), 92 ; Tegid and Gwallter Mechain, ed., *Gwaith Lewis Glyn Cothi* (Oxford, 1837), p. 376.

Dafydd ap Gutun was the great-grandson of Ieuan Gethin. Cyffin is one of his ancestors.

Arundel's land : The Earl of Arundel held the manor of Croesoswallt.

The Coverlet. Jones, 93 ; Mechain, p. 437.

Elin was the daughter of Llywelyn ab Hwlcyn of Llwydiarth in Anglesey. Cynfrig ap Dafydd was her third husband, Prysaddfed their estate in Anglesey. Mahallt, daughter of Hywel Selau, is an ancestress of Elin ; Cynddelw is either an ancestor or a complimentary allusion to the great twelfth-century poet of that name.

Elen of hosts : see 'Sarn Elen' in the glossary.

Lament for Siôn y Glyn. *BYU* 19.

twirling taper : see the note on Dafydd ap Gwilym's 'The Sword'.

DAFYDD NANMOR, *fl.*1450–80. He was said to have been exiled from North Wales because of his love for Gwen o'r Ddôl, and to have settled in the south, where his patrons were the family of Rhys ap Maredudd.

The Peacock. Thomas Roberts, ed., *The Poetical Works of Dafydd Nanmor* (Cardiff and London, 1923), xxvi.

Lament for Gwen. *BYU* 40.

a horned ox : an allusion to Hugh the Strong's oxen, one of which died of grief for its mate.

Nobility. *BYU* 12, *OBWV* 78.

The poem is addressed to Rhys, the son of Rhydderch of Tywyn and the grandson of Rhys ap Maredudd.

as an heir's nursed : the boys of noble families were customarily raised at the courts of other noblemen.

your chin burdened : when you are old enough to have a beard.

RHYS GOCH ERYRI, *c.* 1385–*c.* 1448. His work should be placed, as the dates indicate, earlier in this anthology, but I thought it more effective to place the poem to the fox after Dafydd Nanmor's to the peacock. I must add that because of the dates, Rhys' authorship of that poem is often questioned.

The Fox. *IGE* cix.

The Vision of St. Beuno. *IGE* cvi.

LLYWELYN AP GUTUN, *fl.*1450–70.

The Drowning of Guto'r Glyn. *BYU* 21.

Take, all of you : This poem, and Guto's reply, have as their setting the Christmas festivities of noble households.

a sea-spirit : presumably a reference to Guto's ghost coming from the sea, which will be ousted by Gwido (*see* Glossary).

Pinning the chair : the symbol of the chief bard.

It's not the one-time Guto : directed presumably at Guto, present as the poem was sung.

GUTO'R GLYN, *fl.*1450–90. He was a supporter of the Yorkists during the Wars of the Roses, especially of the Herbart family, and died at the monastery of Valle Crucis, old and blind.

The Drunken Dream of Llywelyn. *BYU* 22.

His nails : in playing the harp.

Llywelyn's sons : a reference to Llywelyn ap Hwlcyn of Anglesey, father of Huw Lewis and father-in-law of Cynfrig ap Dafydd.

the shore he left : his own estate at Melwern.

Wiliam Herbart. *OBWV* 70 ; Ifor Williams and John Llywelyn Williams, eds., *Gwaith Guto'r Glyn* (Cardiff, 1939), xlviii.

Lament for Llywelyn ap y Moel. *OBWV* 72, *Gwaith* v.

Mary's apples : a variety of apple.

Seth's service : an allusion to a popular medieval legend. Seth, sent by his dying father Adam to plead for oil from the tree of mercy in Eden as a curative, is told by an angel that the oil will not be had until Christ's redemption. In the fourteenth-century English poem, *Cursor Mundi*, this legend is interwoven with that of the Rood : Seth sees the tree withered, but has a vision of the infant Christ at its top, and is told that Christ is the oil of mercy ; he is given three seeds of the apple Adam tasted to place under Adam's tongue when he is buried in the Vale of Hebron, from which springs the tree of the Crucifixion. The fullest treatment of the story in Celtic literature is in fourteenth-century Cornish drama: see F. E. Halliday, trans., *The Legend of the Rood* (London, 1955).

Sheep-Dealing. *Gwaith* xxxi.

the tithe : the sheep, which were the parson's tithe.

Y Cwm's David : a compliment to Sir Bened, 'the St. David of Y Cwm'.

A Priest's Love. *OBWV* 73, *Gwaith* xciii.

Lament for Siôn ap Madog Pilstwn. *BYU* 18.

Owain's kinsman : His grandmother was Owain Glyn Dŵr's sister.

Hywel the Good's descendant : Siôn's wife Alswn was the daughter of Hywel ab Ifan, descendant of Tudur Trefor, who married Angharad, Hywel Dda's daughter.

T

Petition. *BYU* 17.

eight ancient stones : Stonehenge.

Young Hywel : Ifan's grandson.

The City Life. *Gwaith* lxix.

A tall earl : the Earl of Arundel.

Meditation. *BYU* 8.

The judgment on the rainbow : the Last Judgment, at the second coming of Christ.

Old Age. *BYU* 9.

DAFYDD AB EDMWND, *fl.*1450–80. He systematized Welsh prosody at the Carmarthen eisteddfod (*c.* 1450), increasing the technical difficulties a bard needed to master as a means of safeguarding the privileges of qualified bards.

A Girl's Hair. Williams, ed., *The Burning Tree* 29 ; Thomas Roberts, ed., *Gwaith Dafydd ab Edmwnd* (Bangor, 1914), xiv.

Under the Eaves. *BYU* 39.

Lament for Siôn Eos. *OBWV* 75.

Hywel's law : Welsh law, which would not have exacted the death penalty.

GWERFUL MECHAIN, *c.* 1462–1500 ? The only woman poet of any note in this period.

The Harp. Leslie Harries, ed., *Barddoniaeth Huw Cae Llwyd, Ieuan ap Huw Cae Llwyd, Ieuan Dyfi, a Gwerful Mechain* (M.A. thesis, National Library of Wales, 1933), lxvii.

TUDUR PENLLYN, *c.* 1420–*c.* 1485.

The Outlaw. *OBWV* 89 ; Thomas Roberts, ed., *Gwaith Tudur Penllyn ac Ieuan ap Tudur Penllyn* (Cardiff, 1958), i.

GUTUN OWAIN, *fl.*1460–1500.

The Hounds. *OBWV* 84.

the baron's kinsman : Hywel ap Rhys was a descendant of Owain Glyn Dŵr

Love's Language. *OBWV* 85.

HUW CAE LLWYD, *c.* 1431–1504.

The Cross. *BYU* 3.

the spark : the Holy Eucharist.

TUDUR ALED, *fl.*1480–1526.

The Stallion. *OBWV* 90.

A Plea for Peace. *OBWV* 93 ; T. Gwynn Jones, ed., *Gwaith Tudur Aled* (Cardiff, 1926), lxvi.

The eight cousins who slandered Hwmffre ap Hywel ap Siencyn and his uncles were : (1) Morgan, (2) Wiliam, (3) Tudur Fychan, (4) Siencyn ap Siôn, (5) Siôn, a relation of Hywel Fychan, (6) Wmffre, (7) Gruffudd, related to Iefan and Dafydd, (8) Morgan Siôn. Derwas is noted as a relative of the first three.

The hindmost yoke : the place of greatest importance before the plough, requiring the best oxen.

Three futile frays : 'Three Futile Battles of the Island of Britain :

One of them was the Battle of Goddeu : it was brought about by the cause of the bitch, together with the roebuck and the plover ;

The second was the Action of Ar[f]derydd, which was brought about by the cause of the lark's nest ;

And the third was the worst, that was Camlan, which was brought about because of a quarrel between Gwen-hwyfar and Gwennhwy[f]ach.' Rachel Bromwich, ed. and trans., *Trioedd Ynys Prydein : The Welsh Triads* (Cardiff, 1961), p. 206. As Miss Bromwich notes, Tudur has apparently confused the causes of the second and third battles.

Love's Frustration. *Gwaith* cxxix.

the Virgins : who went, according to the *Brut*, to be wives in Brittany.

the eleven thousand : the virgins martyred with St. Ursula.

WILIAM LLŶN. Died 1580.

Lament for Sir Owain ap Gwilym. *OBWV* 98.

Hind ox of altars : The hind ox bears the heaviest burden, and is therefore the best. Owain was a priest as well as a bard.

SIÔN TUDUR. Died 1602. He served for a time as a member of Queen Elizabeth's bodyguard, and claimed at the end of his life that he was the oldest living bard.

The Bards. *OBWV* 112.

The Nag. T. Gwynn Jones, ed., *Llên Cymru*, vol. iii (Aberystwyth, 1926), p. 55.

TOMOS PRYS, c. 1564–1634. He fought in the Netherlands under the Earl of Leicester, and was at Tilbury in the army raised against the Armada. He fought in France, Spain, Scotland, and Ireland, and went buccaneering on the Spanish coast.

The Porpoise. Williams, ed., *The Burning Tree*, 45 ; William Rowlands, ed., *Barddoniaeth Tomos Prys o Blasiolyn* (M.A. thesis, National Library of Wales, 1912), xxxiv.

HUW LLWYD. 1568?–1630?

The Fox. *OBWV* 119.

SIÔN PHYLIP. Died 1620.

The Seagull. *OBWV* 118 ; W. J. Gruffydd, ed., *Y Flodeugerdd Newydd* (Cardiff, 1909), p. 203.

From the east spews fresh water : the river Mawddach, at Barmouth.

The flood that runs to Rhuddallt : This reading of the line, which differs from either of the texts cited, was suggested by Mr. D. J. Bowen. The third flood would then be the sea as it enters and flows up the Mawddach in the storm, and it is compared to the Deluge in the following line. This seems to me more effective than the usual reading, which makes the Deluge the third.

GLOSSARY

I HAVE glossed the names of persons and places only when this was necessary to clarify the poems or seemed of special interest. The reader who wishes more geographical and biographical information should consult William Rees's *An Historical Atlas of Wales* (Cardiff, 1951) and *The Dictionary of Welsh Biography* (London, 1959), edited by John Edward Lloyd and R. T. Jenkins.

ANGHARAD. A beautiful and generous woman of the twelfth century, daughter of Owain ab Edwin, a chieftain of eastern Gwynedd.

ANNWN. The underworld in Welsh myth.

AUSTIN. Augustine. There are two St. Augustines, the famous Latin Father (354–430), and the missionary who brought Christianity to the Anglo-Saxons in 596.

AWDL. The term is used for a number of verse forms among the twenty-four 'strict metres' of medieval Welsh poetry.

AWGRIM STONES. 'Algorism' is the Arabic system of numerals. The stones were used for counting.

BELI. Sixth-century ruler of north-west Wales.

BEUNO. A Welsh saint of the seventh century, widely commemorated in North Wales.

BRABANT CLOTH. Fabric made at Lyre or Lierre in Brabant, a province of Belgium.

BRAGGET. A malt drink, containing beer and honey.

BRUT. The Welsh translation (three different ones were made) of Geoffrey of Monmouth's Latin *History of the Kings of Britain* (1136).

BRYCHAN YRTH. A ruler of south-east Wales (Breconshire), father of St. Dwyn.

BWA BACH. 'The little hunchback', Morfudd's husband. 'It is worth while pointing out that a man nicknamed "Y Bwa Bychan" was living in the neighbourhood of Aberystwyth in 1344. . . . Thus Dafydd's name "Y Bwa Bach" is not wholly imaginary.' (Parry, *Welsh Literature*, p. 106.)

BWRD. One of the knights of the Round Table.

CAE GWRGENAU. The name of a noble family's mansion at Nannau in Merioneth.

CAER WYSG. Usk.

CAERNARVON. The castle in north-west Wales was often used as a prison in the Middle Ages.

CAMLAN. The disastrous final battle of Arthur.

CAMLET. A light, expensive fabric.

CARREG CENNEN. A castle in Carmarthenshire.

CERI. A district in Powys, on the English border.

CHEAP. Cheapside, the famous London market.

CROESOSWALLT. Oswestry.

CUHELYN. The Welsh name of the Irish hero, Cuchulain. There was a thirteenth-century Welsh lord of this name.

CURIG. A saint of sixth-century Wales, composer of several hymns.

CYRSEUS. The sword of Otwel, one of Charlemagne's warriors.

DAFYDD AB IEUAN AB IORWERTH. Abbot of Glynegwestl, and later Bishop of St. Asaph. Died 1503.

DAFYDD AP SIANCYN. From his base at Carreg-y-Gwalch, near Llanrwst, he raided the surrounding country and kept the Yorkist forces out of Nanconwy until 1468.

DAVID. The patron saint of Wales, who lived in the latter half of the sixth century.

DEHEUBARTH. South Wales.

DEIFR. A maiden of Arthur's court, noted for beauty.

DEINIOEL. A saint of the early sixth century, founder of the monastery at Bangor.

DEIRA. The ancient Saxon kingdom in north-eastern England.

DERFEL. Derfel the Strong, patron saint of Llandderfel.

DWYN. A saint of the fifth century, patroness of lovers.

DYFED. The ancient kingdom in south-western Wales.

DYFI. The river Dovey in central Wales.

DYFR. See Deifr.

EDEIRNION. A region of north-east Wales.

EDNYFED. Her daughter, Angharad, was Ifan Fychan's wife.

EFROG. The sixth king of ancient Britain.

EFYRNWY. A river in north-eastern Wales, flowing into the Severn.

EIDDIG. 'The Jealous One', the name given by the bards to their ladies' husbands.

EIGR. The wife of Uthr Pendragon and mother of Arthur, renowned for her beauty.

EINION. Identity unknown.

EINIORT. Identity uncertain. Gwyn Williams suggests Eilhart (*The Burning Tree*, p. 115).

ELFFIN. Patron of Taliesin in the sixth century.

ELUCIDARIUM. An eleventh-century religious treatise very popular in the Middle Ages and translated into Welsh *c.* 1200.

ENGLYN. A term used for a number of stanza forms among the 'strict metres'.

ENID. A maiden of Arthur's court, noted for beauty.

ERYRI. Snowdonia.

EUAS. A region in north-eastern Wales.

EURON. Llywelyn ap y Moel's mistress.

FLORA. The Roman goddess of nature.

GARWY. A legendary warrior and lover.

GERAINT AB ERBIN. One of Arthur's warriors. His ferocity in war is depicted in an early poem (see Gwyn Williams's *The Burning Tree,* p. 43).

GLYN EGWESTL. The monastery of Valle Crucis, in north-eastern Wales.

GRIORS. A game, the nature of which is not known.

GWENDDYDD. A woman linked with Merlin, either as sister or lover.

GWENT. South-eastern Wales.

GWENWYNWYN. One of the two divisions of Powys, in north-eastern Wales.

GWGON AP MEURIG. Ninth-century ruler of Cardigan.

GWIDO. According to stories popular after his death in 1324, his ghost walked as punishment for not having done enough penance in this life, and created a disturbance in his widow's house to ensure that she suffered sufficiently before her death.

GWYN AP NUDD. The king of the fairies (*tylwyth teg*) in Welsh myth.

GWYNEDD. North-western Wales.

HAWT-Y-CLYR. The sword of Oliver in *The Song of Roland.*

HERBART, WILIAM. He was knighted by Henry VI in 1449, and fought against Jasper Tudor in the Wars of the Roses. He was made chief justice of South Wales by Edward IV in 1461, of North Wales in 1467, and was created Earl of Pembroke in 1468 after the capture of Harlech Castle. See Howell T. Evans, *Wales and the Wars of the Roses* (Cambridge, 1915).

HORSA. One of the leaders of the Anglo-Saxon invasion of Britain in the fifth century.

HUGH THE STRONG. The Emperor of Constantinople in a twelfth-century French romance about Charlemagne.

HYWEL FYCHAN. Identity uncertain.

HYWEL THE GOOD. Hywel Dda (*c.* 900–950) brought much of Wales under his rule. He is traditionally credited with the codification of Welsh law.

IÂL. A region in north-eastern Wales.

IFOR HAEL. Ifor ap Llywelyn, of Basaleg in South Wales. 'Hael' means 'generous' in Welsh.

INDEG. A beautiful woman in early Welsh romance, one of Arthur's loves.

IS CONWY. A region in North Wales.

ISEULT. Tristan's beloved. 'Iseult's chaplet' (*cae Esyllt*) takes its origin from the medieval practice of bestowing garlands or chaplets on their lovers, and comes to mean simply anything much prized.

KAI. One of Arthur's knights : 'when it pleased him he would be as tall as the tallest tree in the forest' ('Culhwch and Olwen', *The Mabinogion*, p. 107).

LORD RICHMOND. Henry Tudor, Earl of Richmond, who defeated Richard III and became King Henry VII in 1485. Jasper Tudor, Earl of Pembroke, was his uncle.

LLANDDWYN. The church of St. Dwyn in Anglesey.

LLAWDDEN. A fifteenth-century bard.

LLŶR. The god of the sea in Welsh myth.

LLYWARCH HEN. The subject of a number of ninth-century poems, one of which is an elegy to his son Gwên. A portion of this is translated in Gwyn Williams, *An Introduction to Welsh Poetry*, pp. 33–35.

LUNED. A beautiful maiden in Welsh romance.

MADOG HIR. Identity unknown.

MAELOR. A region on the north-eastern border of Wales, divided into Welsh Maelor and English Maelor.

MAIG. An ancient ruler of Powys.

MALLTRAETH. A region in Anglesey.

MANGNEL. A type of catapult. (The usual English word is 'mangonel'.) Its arm was wooden, and when old, lost its spring.

MARCH. The March is the borderland between Wales and England.

MASTER YWAIN. Identity uncertain. Possibly one of the Tudors.

MEIRION. Merioneth.

MELWERN. The home of Llywelyn ap Gutun, near Croesoswallt (Oswestry) in north-eastern Wales.

MENW. A magician, who plays a part in the story of 'Culhwch and Olwen', contained in *The Mabinogion*.

MÔN. Anglesey.

MORDAF. A legendary generous lord.

MORGANNWG. Glamorgan.

NON. A saint of the sixth century, mother of St. David.

NUDD. A legendary generous lord.

NYF. Identity unknown, but clearly she is a beautiful woman alluded to in the same way as Indeg or Deifr. 'Nyf' as an ordinary noun means 'snow'.

OFFA'S DYKE. Offa (757–796) was king of Mercia in central England; the dyke, or earthwork, constructed after a Welsh attack in 784, ran along the border from near Prestatyn in the north to the mouth of the Wye in the south. It seems to have been constructed as a boundary between Wales and Mercia rather than a defence. It became for the Welsh a symbol of the division between Wales and England.

OTWEL. One of Charlemagne's warriors.

OWAIN. The traditional name of the hoped-for liberator of Wales. Llywelyn ap y Moel is probably alluding to this rather than to Owain Glyn Dŵr.

OWAIN GLYN DŴR. Better known to English readers as Owen Glendower (c. 1354–1416). He was descended, as Iolo Goch stresses, from the princes of Powys on his father's side, from those of Deheubarth on his mother's. He fought for Richard II at Berwick in 1385, but rose against Henry IV in 1400. He reached the peak of his success in 1405, with most of Wales in his control, but was decisively defeated in 1408. His great manor at Sycharth was burned to the ground in 1403. See John Edward Lloyd, *Owen Glendower* (Oxford, 1931).

OWAIN WAED DA. A fourteenth-century bard.

PEREDUR. Better known to non-Welsh readers as Perceval or Parsifal in Arthurian romance.

POWYS. North-eastern Wales, divided into Powys Wenwynwyn and Powys Fadog.

PYRS GRUFFUDD. He was from Penrhyn in Caernarvonshire, and seems to have dissipated his estate by 1622. He died in 1628.

RHEINALLT. Possibly Hywel ap Rheinallt, a North Wales bard of the late fifteenth century.

RHYS BWTLWNG. Identity uncertain. Possibly a singer who won the prize at the Carmarthen eisteddfod about 1450.

ROBIN NORDD. 'The Cardigan Assize Roll of 1344 gives us the story of one Robert le Northern, a wealthy burgess of Aberystwyth. . . . This is undoubtedly Dafydd's Robin Nordd. His wife, being an Englishwoman no doubt, would speak Welsh with an accent, as Dafydd says.' Thomas Parry, 'Dafydd ap Gwilym', *Yorkshire Celtic Studies*, v (University of Leeds), pp. 23–24.

ROWENA. The daughter of Hengist, one of the leaders of the fifth-century Anglo-Saxon invasion of Britain.

SANTIAGO. The shrine of St. James at Compostella in Spain, a popular goal of medieval pilgrims.

SARN ELEN. In 'The Dream of Macsen Wledig', the Roman emperor Macsen marries a North Wales princess, Elen, and 'Elen thought to make high roads from one stronghold to another across the Island of Britain. And the roads were made. And for that reason they are called the Roads of Elen of the Hosts, because she was sprung from the Island of Britain, and the men of the Island of Britain would not have made those great hostings for any save for her.' *The Mabinogion*, p. 85.

SAUL. St. Paul.

SIR FULKE. Fulke Fitz Warine, a hero in French romance.

SIR HYWEL. He achieved fame in the French wars of Edward III at Crécy and Poitiers, and was appointed Constable of Criccieth in 1359. He died *c.* 1381.

SIR OWAIN AP GWILYM. A sixteenth-century poet and priest.

SULIEN. An eleventh-century bishop of St. David's, famed for his learning.

TALIESIN. A sixth-century bard.

TEGAU. A beautiful maiden of Arthur's court.

TEGEINGL. A region in north-eastern Wales.

TEIRTUD. 'The harp of Teitu. . . . When a man pleases, it will play of itself; when one would have it so, it is silent' ('Culhwch and Olwen', *The Mabinogion*, p. 115).

TEWDWS TOWER. The Milky Way.

TIBOETH. The book of St. Beuno, the cover of which is said to have been decorated with black jewels.

TRAHAEARN. A noble family of North Wales.

TREFOR. A region in north-eastern Wales.

TWRCH TRWYTH. The great boar that must be hunted as one of the tasks in 'Culhwch and Olwen': 'that day until evening the Irish fought with him ; nevertheless he laid waste one of the five provinces of Ireland' (*The Mabinogion*, p. 131).

URIEN. A sixth-century ruler, celebrated by Taliesin.

UTHR. The father of Arthur in Welsh legend.

UWCH AERON. A region of central Wales.

YNYR. The thirteenth-century ancestor of a powerful noble family at Nannau in Merioneth.

YSTRAD FFLUR. Strata Florida, a Cistercian monastery in central Wales.

YSTRAD MARCHELL. Strata Marcella, a Cistercian monastery in north-eastern Wales.

YSTUDFACH. A bard of the earlier Middle Ages.

Y WAUN. Chirk.

PRINTED BY R. & R. CLARK, LTD., EDINBURGH